Lessons Learned from Occult Letters

Lessons Learned from Occult Letters

William G. Gray

THE SANGREAL SODALITY PRESS
Johannesburg, Gauteng, South Africa

First edition, 2018
First printing, 2018

Published by The Sangreal Sodality Press
74 Twelfth Street
Parkmore 2196
Gauteng
South Africa
Email: jacobsang@gmail.com

Copyright © 2018 Jacobus G. Swart

All rights reserved. No part of this publication may be reproduced or transmitted in any form or by any means, electronic or mechanical, including photocopy, without permission in writing from the publisher. Reviewers who wish to quote brief passages in connection with a review written for inclusion in a magazine, newspaper or broadcast need not request permission.

ISBN 978-0-620-79024-6

Emil Napoleon Hauenstein

(Photo and Cover Image courtesy of Marcus Claridge:
Warden of the Sangreal Sodality in Great Britain)

Contents

Introduction by Jacobus G. Swart i
Prologue 1
The Letters 19
   Letter 1 & 2 19
      Comment 20
   Letter 3 23
      Comment 26
   Letter 4 29
      Comment 30
   Letter 5 33
      Comment 35
   Letter 6 41
      Comment 42
   Letter 7 51
      Comment 52
   Letter 8 61
      Comment 62
   Letter 9 73
      Comment 74
   Letter 10 83
      Comment 85
   Letter 11 95
      Comment 96
   Epistle 1 105
      Comment 106
   Epistle 2 115
      Comment 118
Epilogue 127

INTRODUCTION
by
Jacobus G. Swart

William G. Gray wrote "*Lessons Learned from Occult Letters*" in 1949. Four years have passed since the conclusion of World War II, and nine since the "Battle of Dunkirk," an event which turned him inside out from top to bottom, transformed his perception regarding the meaning of life, and made him revalue everything.

He penned this, his very first book, at the age of 33, a decade prior to the demise of Emil Napoleon Hauenstein, his friend and mentor, who passed away in September 1959 at the age of 78 years from cancer of the liver. Contrary to opinions expressed regarding Hauenstein's status as a "Magus," it should be noted that he was nothing of the sort. Whilst he was an "Initiate" of the well-known French Occultist Papus (Gerard Encausse), he had a particularly poor opinion of ritual magic, and stated this plainly enough to William Gray who confirmed Hauenstein's stance in the many letters he wrote me. In fact, Hauenstein believed magical abilities unfold automatically as individuals develop higher spiritual faculties. Hence he distrusted the teaching of magic since, in his opinion, true magic could not be taught.

E.N.H., as William Gray affectionately called Emil Napoleon Hauenstein, classified himself a "mystic," specifically a "Christian Mystic," and in this regard it should be noted that he was a Martinist. It was through the *L'Ordre Kabbalistique de la Rose Croix* (Kabbalistic Order of the Rosy Cross) and "Martinism" that E.N.H. met Papus. Martinism was a lot more popular in continental Europe than in Britain, and it is rather "Christian" in content, though *mystically* so. This tradition does not have a lot of ritual, and is mainly ethical and meditational. So, as far as William Gray's particular predilection for Ritual Magic is concerned, Hauenstein tried to dissuade him from travelling the magical path and persistently insisted on direct prayers rather than elaborate ceremonies. William Gray and Hauenstein never saw eye to eye on that point. E.N.H. admitted that ceremonies had great potency, but only in cases where everyone involved knew how to handle them.

Emil Napoleon Hauenstein's link with Martinism was via it's 20th century American "sister order" named AMORC, the *"Ancient Mystical Order Rosae Crucis,"* which he was very enthusiastic about. In fact, most of the spiritual techniques he addressed in the letters shared in this tome, were derived directly from the curriculum of this "Order." William Gray, then a youngster with no practical experience but having considerable intuition, kept insisting that AMORC was only a moneymaking American business concern. They had endless arguments about this. E.N.H., who was Austrian, would use logic in a truly Teutonic way to show how his young friend could not be "*Korrekt*" without personal experience, since he was working purely from "inner instinct."

Eventually he had to admit William Gray was right, though he kept insisting how AMORC taught solely the very best ethical principles. Doubtless they did, but, as far as William Gray was concerned, their "first principle" was money. Of course, it is perfectly clear that *any* organisation with a physical presence in this world needs cold cash, and the more elaborate it gets the more money is required. However, when spiritual principles are involved, money should never be the first, but the last consideration. Sadly, far too many "Occult Schools" make it the first, and this is what William Gray was on about. Of course, he was not "anti" any esoteric institution *per se*, after all, he was at one time a member of Dion Fortune's *"Society and Fraternity of the Inner Light."*

It was through this esoteric fraternity that William Gray met Basil Wilby, in whose ideas of occult publishing he became interested. Wilby is the Western Esoteric author who writes under the *nom-de-plume* "Gareth Knight." He was one of the partners in Helios who published several esoteric works. They released William Gray's *"The Ladder of Lights,"* and a number of his other tomes which are now considered classics in their field. Interestingly enough, William Gray wrote the said work purely as study matter on Kabbalah for his personal students. In fact, he informed me that he wrote this work at the prompting of one particular member of his circle, who could not make much sense of the other Kabbalistic books available then. He also wrote it to more or less clarify his own ideas about the kabbalistic Tree of Life. Later he showed the manuscript to Wilby who, I understood, cautiously tried it on Israel Regardie who did not only react favourably, but apparently told Basil Wilby it was likely to prove a winner. In turn, Regardie showed the *"Ladder of Lights"* to Carr Collins, an American sponsor, who got in touch with William Gray with an offer to back the publication of the book with Helios. The rest is history.

William Gray's major works started to appear around two decades after his first tentative steps in writing down the burgeoning esoteric notions expressed in *"Lessons Learned from Occult Letters."* Many of the "scientific" notions addressed in this tome, whether these be of the physical or occult varieties, are in harmony with the perspectives prevalent in the 1940's, but whilst many readers may prefer perusing the fully matured esoteric doctrines and occult practices addressed in his later writings, I believe the current tome affords readers an insight into the remarkable companionship between William Gray and his mentor. E.N.H. gently encouraged his, perhaps somewhat "tempestuous," *protegé* along the "ways of truth and goodness," doing so without making undue demands or interference as far as "Free Will" is concerned.

In the end, William Gray became the "Ceremonial Magician," accepting ritualised practice as a convenience for coordinating consciousness. Yet, perusing the letters which passed between him and E.N.H., as well as the running commentary accompanying each of these, it is clear that the "Pupil" indeed "Learned" numerous "Lessons" from the "Occult Letters" of his "Master," who passed the authority of his "Line of Light" to William Gray with the words:

"This life is rather like a relay race where the next runner picks up a baton from the last one and carries on. Well, you're the next one along this line, so take up the rod I'm passing you and bear it as far as you can go before you have to pass it along yourself, and hope it goes into good hands." [William G. Gray: *My Autobiography* (unpublished manuscript, facsimile copy, Sangreal Sodality Archives, Temple Lux Occidentis in Extensio, Johannesburg, South Africa)]

Jacobus G. Swart
Warden: The Sangreal Sodality®
Johannesburg
February 2018

PROLOGUE

First interests in "Occult" subjects, are likely to have very far-reaching effects on anyone's life, and especially so when one happens to be physically young in years. For that reason, it is of great importance that such interests may have the best and most helpful effect upon the person concerned. Otherwise, it is no exaggeration to say that a whole life may be wretchedly spoiled, or at least made unhappy and unfruitful.

What follows, is meant to help those who like myself became deeply interested in the Occult at an early age, and still are young in body. Perhaps it may help those who are physically older, but whose Occult interests are recent. In any case, I sincerely hope that others may profit at the expense of my own mistakes and experiences, and may be helped and guided as I was, even though I did not appreciate that guidance at the time it was given me. After all, what is the use of making mistakes and being helped through them, if one does not pass on that help and information to someone else for their benefit?

Let us start with Occultism itself. What exactly does it mean anyhow? So many people say and write different things about it, that it is apt to be a most muddle-some word. Literally of course, as one soon learns, it means "hidden." In other words, something unknown to oneself. This carries the implication that an Occultist is a person who seeks to find out knowledge which is hidden from them at the time they decide to look for it. Since this could apply to a student of any subject at all, we need to qualify the word "Occult" still further, and decide what *sort* of knowledge it refers to.

Generally speaking, Occult knowledge is a knowledge of that which is, as it were, "behind" everything. That is to say, with causes of effects throughout Nature in every sense. The Occultist is a deep enquirer into everything, who accepts no ordinary limits to the depth of his enquiries. For instance, if one says "Electricity is a behaviour of electrons," the Occultist immediately asks "Well then, and what *are* electrons?" Tell him that they are so far as we know the smallest particles of matter, and he then says "Yes, and what *is* matter?" Here, even the greatest of our physical scientists become vague. They can talk all round the subject, and explain what matter *does* with wonderful precision, yet they cannot say exactly and precisely what it *is*. This does not satisfy the Occultist at all, and so, being insatiable for knowledge, he tries to get *beyond* Matter, and find out what is "behind" it. Whatever he finds out, he attempts to "get behind" in turn, and so he goes along.

Hence, the main field of an Occultist's interest and activities lies "behind" and "outside of" ordinary material things and circumstances. He starts his work where the physical scientist has to leave off for want of material. That means to say that the Occultist must develop senses within himself which are able to deal with conditions which are "beyond" the normal material happenings of this world. He must train himself just as much, and indeed more so, as if he were qualifying to take a degree at any University. His course of study is of a much longer period, and the examinations he has to pass are practically continuous. He must, as I was told myself, "become a living question mark" if he is to succeed at the enormous task he has set himself.

Occultism then, is the study and practice of subjects and laws which are beyond the bounds and limitations of ordinary physical or even mental experience. Since those subjects and laws are hidden from our normal senses which cannot respond to them, they may justifiably be called "Occult."

The point is, why should anyone study Occultism at all? What good can it do for human beings? What is its purpose? Why should you want to associate yourself with it? All these questions have to be answered, or there is no point at all in concerning yourself with Occultism. Unless you can provide some reasonable answers, you had far better leave Occultism altogether alone until you feel more sure of yourself.

Every human being who claims to be "interested in the Occult" must answer those questions for themselves, because upon the nature of their own answers, depends their individual attitude to the "Occult." Supposing, however, that one had to provide a set of answers as an example, one could well do so along these lines.

The study of Occultism is justified or condemned by the use to which it is put by its students. If they study it for a good purpose, to help themselves become better and more advanced people, and for the benefit of all living creatures besides themselves as well, then that is a good reason for concerning themselves with Occult matters. If, on the other hand, they want to gain knowledge for selfish and evil purposes so that they can do what they like at the expense and suffering of everyone else, then their reason for studying Occultism is the worst possible one, and can lead to nothing but harm and misery all round.

The reason why one studies Occultism at all, is simply because it enables us to live and adjust our lives in accordance with laws and forces which affect us in the closest possible way, even though they are non-physical in nature. The more we know about any force or law which affects our existence, the better we can make that existence of ours if we avail ourselves of our knowledge. On the other hand, knowledge can be a very dangerous possession in the hands of an unscrupulous and evilly disposed person. That is why so called "Occult secrets" *are* kept secret so far as possible by those in authorised possession of them. Anyone can do enough harm as it is, by a knowledge of purely physical poisons and scientific formulas. Think of the incredible harm and evil that could be done by the misapplication of mental and spiritual laws, and you will see why knowledge of those laws is not made public. A good example of such a misapplication was Nazi Germany, and just consider the sufferings and horrors let loose in the world thereby.

Supposing for instance, that someone has sufficient knowledge of Occult laws to enable him to influence and seriously affect the minds and souls of other people. If he were an irresponsible or an evil person, he could do an amazing amount of damage and injury all round him before a stop might be put to his activities. He might easily drive people mad, or to crimes which they would not otherwise have committed. He would also injure himself morally, mentally, and possibly even physically into the bargain. Consequently, it is of the greatest importance that before anyone gains "Occult powers," they should be made fit to use and handle them.

Occult powers are very real indeed, and they can be used for either good or evil ends. They roughly consist of the ability to direct and control according to one's will, the forces which lie within the range of the mind and soul. By their means, even unusual physical phenomena can be produced, and so called "miracles" take place. These forces are as real, and much more powerful than steam, electricity, magnetism, or any other power producing physical results. Our minds and souls are *real*, and exist, even though we are not usually very conscious of them while we live in physical bodies. Moreover, they are infinitely more important to us than our physical bodies, since they are the immortal part of ourselves in which we live when our physical bodies are "dead." All study of principles, powers and forces which affect those parts of ourselves, is therefore of the highest importance to us, and can influence us tremendously for either good or ill.

Why should knowledge of such things be especially confined to "Occultism"? The answer to that is a simple question: In what other branch of study can it be found? Physical science does not claim to deal with either minds, souls, or anything at all that is not purely material. Psychology goes a step further, and deals in the behaviour of the human mind up to a point, but dislikes admitting the positive existence of other states of being than the material existence on this earth. Orthodox religion teaches the immortal nature of mankind, and expounds many excellent and necessary spiritual truths for the guidance of human life and behaviour, but it does not teach the modus operandi by which spiritual and mental forces can be handled by humanity. This is where Occultism comes in, making a positive assertion that the "hidden laws" and "secret forces" behind our ordinary beings are first of all in actual existence, secondly that they are there to be used consciously by ourselves when we reach a state of development when this will be possible to us, and moreover, that we can only progress in evolution and become more perfect than we are, by the action of those superphysical forces within us.

Notice that word "conscious." It is the key to the whole question, for it is by the use of our consciousness that we have become what we are already, and what we shall be in the future depends upon how we employ this highest faculty of ours and the power it enables us to control. The better our consciousness becomes, the better we can become ourselves. This is the aim of Occult study, to improve and increase our consciousness far beyond our present range so that we shall be able to deal with spiritual, mental, and other non-physical forces and states of existence which we are not aware of in our "ordinary" or "everyday" consciousness.

If you like to think of it this way, Occultism is a means of human development so that we can make progress along definite and systematic lines, and therefore get far better and more rapid results than if we simply "let things take their course." Roughly speaking, the difference between an Occultist and a non-Occultist, is about the same as that between a *trained* musician, and one who just "picked up playing as they went along." Both people can *play*, but what a difference there will be between the two performances! So with Occultism. Everybody can be conscious, but what an enormous difference there is between a *trained* consciousness along any line, and one that has merely "fiddled around with the subject." That is the purpose of Occultism, to *train* and *educate* our consciousness so that it becomes able to function and operate on increasingly higher levels, and in consequence we become more and more advanced in nature as we go along.

How does Occult training work? Very much the same as any other sort of training. The trainee has to profit by the experience and teaching of those who have gone before him and who have reached the conscious level of which he hopes some day to reach himself. He has to study and apply himself to what they can teach him and put their lessons into the terms of his own experience. He has to practice the exercises he is given and make himself a "good pupil" in every sense of the term. Furthermore, he has to pass "exams" before he is able to "go to a higher class." In a way, it is all very similar to a University except that instead of being "graduated" one becomes "Initiated."

In olden times, there actually were "Schools of Initiation" which selected pupils could attend and be trained in. Nowadays, the position is very different, and one cannot simply approach a "School of Initiation" and apply for a prospectus. Nor do Masters and Adepts of the Occult put brass plates on their doors stating their qualifications and inviting prospective pupils. Why is this? Is there any less need for Occultism than there was two thousand and more years ago? On the contrary, there is as much need today as there ever has been — indeed more, only the system is very much altered in the present time.

For one thing, the consciousness of humanity in general has made enormous strides in twenty centuries. Methods producing good results two thousand odd years ago are not applicable today. Another point to take into consideration is that under modern Western conditions we cannot very well enter Schools of Initiation and give up our entire lives to the study of Occult arts. Our self-imposed social and economic conditions alone make that out of the question except for people with unearned incomes having some type of "independent means." It would obviously be totally unfair to restrict Occult study to such people alone. Therefore the whole plan of Initiation had to be modified and brought "up to date," at least so far as Westerners are concerned. How then, does it work, and what are our chances of Occult study, progress, and Initiation?

Seeing the trend of Western civilisation, and the advancement in our consciousness, as also for other reasons, the "Powers that Be" behind the Occult teachings and traditions in this world, decided upon a peculiar course. During the last hundred years, they caused quite a large amount of Occult knowledge to be generally released throughout the Western world, so that anyone who cared to study it could do so. A tremendous amount of "Occult" books were written, or translated from hitherto unobtainable documents. "Societies" and "Brotherhoods" sprang up all overt the place in Europe, England and America. Interest in Occultism became widespread and public. Occult doctrines and "secrets" that had before that time only been available within closely guarded and concealed "Schools," were given out to the public at last. The purpose of all this was mainly as follows.

Humanity is always faced with the task of working out its own salvation. In its early stages of development individuals capable of making outstanding progress, especially along mental or spiritual lines, were few and far between. They had to be most carefully encouraged and looked after by those of higher development who were capable of doing so. The mass of humanity was not fit to be trusted with knowledge which they would certainly use for evil and irresponsible ends. With the passing of the centuries, this position has been considerably altered, and although humanity is certainly not fit to possess a general working knowledge of Occult secrets with which it might irretrievably ruin itself, yet nevertheless it has advanced to a stage where it can be given a certain amount of knowledge "on trust," in order that it may have the chance of using that knowledge for its own betterment.

It is as though the "Higher Ups" in Occultism said to Humanity in general: "You have got to a stage where you are far better able to look after yourselves than you were some centuries ago. Very well then, here is some knowledge to be going on with, which can do you a lot of good if you care to use it the right way. Of course, it can do you a certain proportion of harm too if you misuse it, but at the same time, you ought to be old and experienced enough to know better. You are getting more and more responsible for your own actions, and so you deserve this much information which will enable you to make your own way along. When you have learned these lessons we have given you, then you shall have some more. We have given you quite enough material for you to initiate yourselves several degrees by your own efforts. Now then, let us see what you can do."

That is roughly our position today. There is quite enough Occult information available for everyone possessed of intelligence and interest to develop himself very considerably indeed. The responsibility of doing so rests with ourselves. Instead of having to attend a "School of Initiation," or become a personal pupil of a "Master," we can learn all the necessary groundwork for ourselves. If we will not bother to make that effort "off our own bat," then we should certainly not be worthy of any "Master" or "School" prepared to receive us when we had made ourselves fit and ready for their attention.

Both "Masters" and "Schools" are still very much in existence, except that today, the standard of "entrance exams" is very much higher than it was a long time ago, and neither "Masters" nor "Schools" can be met with in any ordinary way. The whole idea is that we should develop our spiritual or "Inner" senses until we are capable of recognising for ourselves, who, where, and what the "Schools" and "Masters" really are. They will no longer make overtures to us, it is we who must find them if we want to. We are told that we have the intelligence, ability, and the material to do so for ourselves, and the rest is up to us.

Naturally, we can make very much better progress in an "Occult School" under the tuition of qualified "Masters," than we can outside of such guidance, but on the other hand, if we are too lazy or indifferent to attend to our own primary "education" ourselves, then it would be perfectly useless for us to attend any such "School," and a sheer waste of time for all concerned. It would be just as useless as for someone without even an elementary schooling, to attend the highest type of university lectures.

Now by "Occult Schools" and "Masters" I mean those which are hidden and therefore "Occult," as far as the vast majority of humanity are concerned. There are a very large number of "Brotherhoods," "Groups," "Orders," and all sorts of "Occult" associations which advertise themselves from time to time, and which can be joined in the ordinary way by practically any human being really interested in them. Some of them are good, some bad, and others indifferent according to the people of whom they are composed. Like any other purely human undertaking, they are by no means infallible. Whether to join any of them or not, is a matter to be decided by each individual for themselves. It is safe to say that any really bad, wicked, or evil Occult association would never advertise itself in any public way, for the simple reason that its activities would soon be exposed, and the police would promptly put a very unromantic end to its career. Those "Occult" Brotherhoods and Groups which are at least semi-public, are therefore innocuous enough, and sometimes a very great help. The very worst one could expect to receive at their hands would be a waste of one's time, and very likely money too. It depends largely of course, upon what one *wants* for an expenditure of one's cash and time.

True Occult knowledge is *never* sold for so much money per lesson as though it were some kind of a commodity. Anyone claiming to be an Initiate, or any self styled "Brotherhood" or whatnot, that offers to sell Occult knowledge at so many pounds or dollars per set of instructions, is very definitely a fraud and a sham. You may positively depend on that, and save your money and time accordingly. That sort of thing is absolutely forbidden in any kind of genuine Occult association. It is quite permissible and legitimate of course, if one is a member of any type of Occult "Group" which has an ordinary mundane organisation, to contribute towards the normal working expenses. That is quite another matter. While books, stationary, stamps, and all sorts of material equipment have to be paid for in the usual way, then it is only right and just that the members of the "Groups" who use those things, should foot the bill between them. Everyone should understand that. What knowledge there is to be given, however, must *always* be given *freely* to those considered worthy of having it.

The "Occult Schools" I refer to, are outside of and beyond any ordinary material contacts. When, and if one is ready to enter them, they will be found easily enough, but preparation to enter them is long and difficult. There is an old, and very well known saying in connection with them: "When the pupil is ready, then the Master will appear." Now what exactly does this mean? Actually, it means precisely what it says, and is quite correct as it stands, and yet it has often been hopelessly misinterpreted and distorted by many people who really ought to have more sense.

This phrase: "When the pupil is ready, then the Master will appear," is often taken to mean that one has only to take a certain amount of interest in the Occult, and a wonderful Being simply comes along and invites one to be his personal pupil at some far-away retreat in the Himalayan mountains or equally mysterious place. Far from such immediate promise of romance is the more prosaic but nearer truth. Study the phrase again carefully, and you will find the clue.

In the first place, it does not specify the *kind* of Master who will appear. Nor does it say that the Master will always be personally with you, or that it will be the same Master all the time. For you, a Master is a source of learning and knowledge, strictly speaking therefore, it need not be a human personage at all, but might be even a book, or a piece of information, which would fulfil your immediate needs perfectly well. The word "Master" covers a very wide range indeed.

In fact, some kind of Master will indeed "appear" for you when necessary, during every stage of your Occult development. That is absolutely true, but personal, discipleship where Master and pupil share a common and constant state of consciousness together, only comes when one has reached a comparatively high state of being, where such a kind of tuition will have its very best effect on one, and make all the difference between discipleship and becoming a Master oneself.

Nevertheless, everyone's whole Occult progress is very carefully watched over by those who are able to operate consciously on Spiritual and Mental states of being. At first, while our higher spiritual and mental faculties are as yet unawakened in us, we are not consciously aware of them, though they are very well aware of us and the sort of people we are, since they are able to see us as we cannot see ourselves. So far as we are concerned, we may call them "Masters," or what we please. Some of them may be living in physical bodies somewhere on this earth, and others may be living in quite different sorts of bodies elsewhere. For us, they are a much higher type of being than ourselves, who were once as we are now, and who are trying to help us along the path of our evolution as once they were helped themselves. The only reward they expect is that we too, will extend our help to others in our turn, when we are able to do so.

These "Masters" work in all sorts of ways to help us that we cannot recognise with any of our ordinary senses. Being able to influence the mental and spiritual part of ourselves, they can do a very great deal for us in one way and another. Remember however, that there is one thing they will *never* do, and that is use compulsion on us in any way, shape or form. Our free will is a sacred principle with which they will never interfere in the slightest. Only a Black, or Evil Initiate deliberately seeks to subordinate the will of another human soul entirely to his own. Even he is powerless to *compel* anyone's will, which must be submitted to him by the person themselves of their own accord. No Master, of Good or Evil, has any more authority over a person than they allow that Master to have by their own consent. The Masters may persuade, advise, assist, or take whatever steps they think advisable towards one, but on no account can they *make* one do anything at all that one really and honestly will not do. Nobody can be made good or evil against their own will, no matter what inducements are offered in either direction.

Let us suppose that you have decided to "Take up Occultism," and you naturally expect whatever "Masters" may be watching your efforts from a spiritual viewpoint, to take some interest in you and help you along in some way. I wonder just what you really expect them to do about it? Of course, it does depend entirely upon yourself, yet I do hope you will not be hopelessly disappointed if nothing spectacular or phenomenal appears to happen in your life as an immediate consequence of your Occult interests. Actually, things *will* begin to happen if you can recognise them as being connected with your Occult tendencies, and see them in the light of your own illumination by which they should be regarded. If you can do this, then they will appear to you as they really are — signposts along the path of your progress.

What will happen to you depends absolutely upon the sort of person you are, and also the amount of interest and work which you devote to "Occult" ends. For instance, if you are just "Mildly interested," and simply "like to do a bit of reading about it," then it is most unlikely that anything especial will happen in your life at all. If, on the other hand, you are "very deeply interested indeed," and read, study, and think about Occult subjects as well as *practising* for yourself the principles you read about, then you are simply *bound* to get results of some kind.

These results vary enormously in accordance with individuals, and can be harmful as well as helpful. You may even have most interesting and fascinating "psychic" experiences, *but* the mere fact of having an experience does not prove that it is either good or helpful, so far as you are concerned. Remember the saying "Seek you first the Kingdom of Go(o)d, and these other things shall be added unto you." That is the most valuable maxim to imprint upon yourself as deeply as you can, and no amount of time spent in thinking about it will ever be wasted. Above all else, *be of good purpose*, and mean to do good to the very best of your ability, and then you may be entirely assured that those Masters who are especially concerned with human progress along the Right Hand, or "Good Path," will most certainly help you along, even to the extent of protecting you, so far as they are allowed, from your own mistakes arising through well-meant, though foolish actions.

In the usual course of events, you will most likely consider that nothing very amazing happens because you are following up a line of Occult interests. If this is so, do please remember that it is because you are attempting to analyse your life with your *ordinary* mental senses, just as you were before you "got interested in the Occult." That won't do at all. It is about as much use as trying to receive a radio programme with an electric iron. You are using the wrong instrument. The Masters and their helpers work very much in spiritual, and other superphysical ways which cannot be observed by your ordinary consciousness at all. You will have to look deeper than the surface of things if you want to see "behind" them where the Occult influences are at work.

If you really have decided to make progress on the Occult Path, and are thinking and acting accordingly, all sorts of things and people will come into your life that could not have done so otherwise. Through some of these people and circumstances at least, the Masters will direct their influence towards you. Let us take a few simple examples.

Suppose for instance, that you are working along any particular line of Occult thought and you really need help in developing it. You might easily get into conversation with some newly made acquaintances who could give you that help themselves, or else by lending you a book or introducing you to someone else, the help you needed would be forthcoming. That sort of thing often happens. The thing to ask yourself here, is *why* should anyone or anything come along to help you? Exactly! *Who* sent them, or *how* were you influenced to come in contact? What is the point. Yet such help definitely comes along, often when least expected. The Masters and their helpers may use very ordinary instruments to work with in this physical world, but the *means* by which they persuade those instruments to work as they should, are not of this world itself. In that sense, "when the pupil is ready, then the master will appear," is exceedingly true. When you are ready for, and in real need of Occult teaching, then it will most certainly be given to you in some way. The "Master" in each case, may be, and usually is, entirely different to suit the occasion. The "Master" may for the time being, simply be a friend of yours who knows more than you do and is willing to help you. It may be a casual acquaintance whom you only know for a short time, but who is able to give just the help you need. It may be a book, some happening that makes you think along the right lines, or perhaps an inspirational thought that "flashes into your mind." All such apparently ordinary instances positively come under the heading of "Appearances of the Master to the pupil." Remember that although the instances are ordinary enough in themselves, the fact that they should happen, and do happen, is an *extra*ordinary one. It may seem a strange thing to you, but the Masters use *unusual* means to produce *usual* effects in this world. Now think that out!

Here, please pay close attention. It has been said that when the pupil is ready, and *needs* help, then it will be given. Quite right, but there is a vast difference between *needs* and *wants*. It is most important that you should understand this. What you want, and what you need, are very often two entirely separate things. If everyone wanted exactly what they needed, and nothing else, then the whole world would be a much better place. Far too often we want something which would be very bad for us, and things we really need to make us better than we are, are just those things which we do not want to have. That is just our human foolishness and something we have to put right as we learn better. It is as well for us that we cannot get what we want all the time. A baby, for instance, often *wants* to eat small pieces of coal, but think of the result if the parents allowed it to do so. The same baby may *need* very badly a does of some unpleasant medicine which will correct its ill-health. It will not *want* to swallow the nasty dose, but consider what will happen to its health and well-being, if it does not take the medicine it *needs*. It takes a very long time for human beings to distinguish between what they want and what they need, and when mental and spiritual wants and needs are considered, all of us are capable of making the silliest and sometimes hurtful mistakes. Luckily, the Masters are people who have learned better themselves, and can therefore guide us accordingly.

Now, I have said that Masters never interfere with anyone's free will, and yet at the same time they are often able to stop us from getting something that we want which may be harmful to us. Why is this? It is because our Wills, and our wants, are two different principles entirely. Our Will is something that comes directly from a very high part of our consciousness which knows what it is doing, and means to act as it directs itself. Our *wants* are merely urges in some direction or another, often arising from some lower part of our natures which is in ignorance of what is best for it or any other part of us. *Will* acts positively either for good or evil, in the light of Knowledge and conscious determination, whereas *wants* simply desires something regardless of other considerations. Our Wills are the action of our own Selves and therefore the Masters do not interfere with them. Our wants, however, are simply impulses from some or other part of us, which may actually be working against our Selves' interests. We have to learn how to control these wants and desires, if they are to help instead of hindering us. It is the task of our own Wills, to conquer and control the irresponsible wants which arise in us. This is where the Masters can help us, because if it is our real Will that they would do so, they can often see to it that in our own best interests we do not get something which we merely *want*, but which would do us harm if we got it. Thus, they are not working *against* our wills at all, but *for* them. This may sound like a contradiction of sorts, but it isn't. Careful thinking will soon straighten the matter out once the fundamental difference between *Will* and *want* is understood. It sometimes happens that one has to say to oneself: "I *will* do such and such a thing even though I don't really *want* to, because I know it is the right thing to do, and what is *needed* under the circumstances." That is the whole idea in the proverbial nutshell.

I am going to give a personal example of how this business of Wills, wants, and needs is attended to by the Masters and their helpers. It is a real Occult experience of my own, so I can vouch for its truth, and know that what I am saying will be helpful as an illustration.

When I was in my early 'teens,' and in the stages of being "frantically keen" on Occultism, I saw an advertisement in an Occult magazine which offered a book for sale that I immediately *wanted*, and *desired* very much to possess. Its price was quite beyond my means, and I saw no hopes of getting hold of it. So I decided to use "Occult" means, and performed a little "Magical ceremony" which I calculated might have effect. Nothing happened at all that I could see. No spirits or anything unusual appeared to me whatever, and it looked as though I had entirely wasted my time. Some time later, I had a most unusual and striking "Dream" experience.

I "dreamed," whilst my physical body lay asleep, that I was in a vast library of simply incredible dimensions. It seemed to go up to an amazing height, one book-case on top of another till I could not even make out the ceiling. Galleries ran all round these so that one could get to any book one wanted. I found myself to be on one of these galleries, accompanied by a guide. The curious part is, that I never saw my guide's face, since he always stood slightly behind me, and to one side. I knew him to be a man by his voice, and realised "out of the corner of my eye," that he wore some kind of a deep ruby coloured gown. He seemed full of good humour and was kindness itself.

I remember saying something to him about what a wonderful library it was, and how pleased I was to be there, etc. He replied: "Yes. Do you know that we have every book here that was ever written in the world?" Full of my desire and want for this particular book I have mentioned, I burst out with: "Oh, then you must have so and so's book here. Could I have it please?" Just like that! To my astonishment, he began to laugh quite heartily. "Oh, *that* one! Yes, we even have that. This is it." He stooped down (and I still could not make out his face), and took a volume from a low shelf quite near us. I almost grabbed at it, but he gave it, as I thought, a rather contemptuous flip and dropped it on the ground. "No, leave it there" he said to me as I bent to retrieve it. "It's of no value at all." The dream faded out then, and I woke up remembering it most clearly and was very disappointed about it indeed. It made no sense to me then whatever, and I felt quite disgusted that even someone in a dream should treat a book so rudely that I wanted extremely badly. You see, I was positive even then, that *I* was right, and the dream has been all wrong.

Now for the sequel. In the course of time, I forgot all about the book in question and it just became an almost obliterated memory of something unimportant in the past. Over then years later, a parcel of Occult books was sent as a present to someone I know, who in turn insisted on giving some to me that they felt sure I would be interested in. Yes. The very book in question was among them! It had come into my hands at last in a quite unexpected way. My little "magical" experiment of years ago seemed to have worked eventually. Believe me, I had quite a "queer feeling" as I opened my book! I felt queerer still when I realised what it was all about, and that not only had the "man in my dream" been perfectly right — it was worthless, but also the book could be positively very harmful to anyone trying the Occult experiments in it. Moreover, it was written by a man with a shocking personal record, and who had a very ill repute indeed. He had written it under a high-sounding title, claiming to be a Master, in order to disguise his real identity from the reader. For those reasons, I am not going to mention the title of the book.

That shows how the Masters work. I *wanted* something that would have been very bad for me at the time I wanted it. It might have done me some serious harm then. So I was gently prevented from having it. Much later on, when I had learned better, the book "arrived" at a time when it no longer had any power to affect me, so that my own mistake could be proved to me. Now then, supposing I had not remembered my "Dream" experience? I should not have *consciously* been aware of what really happened. It would have happened just the same, whether I had remembered anything or not, and the result to me in this world would have been the same. My Will, in that case, was that I *wanted* something to help me. Well, thanks to whoever was responsible, I got it, but *not* as I had *desired* or expected it to be. So much the better for me!

That sort of thing can very easily happen to you, or anyone else "Interested in the Occult," except that you might not have any memory of experiences in any other world except the physical one. Such memories are not common, and so you might miss the point of quite a lot of things that happen to you in connection with your Occult interests. Don't make the mistake of thinking that nothing happens just because you are not conscious of all the ins and outs of things. A tremendous amount of happenings take place which affect you very closely, without your being aware of them at all. As you develop your consciousness, you will get to know more about the "inside" workings of Occult forces and intelligences, which influences you without your ordinary conscious knowledge being informed.

Now we come to some more "Occult Workings," and to the substance of this book. It is mainly a series of letters sent to me, when I was a very young man, by a developed and experienced Occultist who wanted to help me. His letters *did* help me far more than I realised at the time. It has recently occurred to me that other people could be helped by these letters too. I therefore asked the writer's permission to publish what he had written to me years ago, and obtained his consent, providing I withheld his name and deleted all personal references. This, I have faithfully done, to the best of my ability, merely editing them in the normal way. One point I would like to make clear, is that I have not withheld any wonderful Occult "secrets" or private information that might have been in the letters. In fact, there was nothing of the kind in them at all. They are given just as he wrote them to me, except that I have corrected his phraseology here and there, since although his command of the English language was excellent, he was not of British origin, and sometimes apt to make odd mistakes and slips.

Prologue / 17

Perhaps you have often wondered about Occultists, and what sort of people they might be in the main. These letters will give you a direct insight into the methods and character of an Initiate who had travelled far, and often painfully along the Path. As he confesses himself, he made many mistakes and errors, and his one thought so far as I was concerned, was to save me from falling into the same traps myself. With that same thought, I pass on what he gave me.

My first contact with him was through an ordinary enough channel in this world, but worked according to the peculiar methods I have spoken about before. What happened was that I felt impressed to write a letter to a certain Occult magazine. The text of the letter I received "Inspirationally," which is to say that it simply "came into my head." At any rate, I sent the letter off, and in due course of time it was published, and being young, I was delighted to see myself in print. Shortly after that I had a note of enquiry from the man whose letters you are now going to read, and altogether we kept up a correspondence for about two years. It is interesting to note that his was the solitary answer to my published letter. Just the person I *needed* to help me, and nobody else!

I have done my best to keep his letters in chronological order, which is a most difficult task, because he rarely dated them. This does not matter very much however, because each letter is complete in itself as it stands, and should, in any case, be considered separately. To give them a kind of continuity, I have added what explanations or enlargements I consider necessary in between them. Listen now, to what a modern Occultist of repute and responsibility had to say to a young man full of his own self importance, and keenly enthusiastic about Occultism as he imagined it to be!

THE LETTERS

LETTER 1 & 2

In answer to my published letter:

Dear Sir,

Having read your letter in the .... magazine, and certainly was impressed by it, I would like to put a few questions to you if convenient, for this concerns me extremely.

With Peace Profound,

I am yours fraternally.

I replied to this, by telling my correspondent that the letter which had been published, was an "inspirational one," mentioned a few facts about myself, etc., and awaited a response. Here it is:

.....Thanking you for your letter, which I received appropriately on New Year's Day, for which I was pleased. To start with, I must introduce myself.....(here follow personal details).....and after a good amount of travels in different countries settled here in England, now for thirty years.

Ever since my youth, I had been attracted to Occultism, and having always had more or less rather a hard life on this plane, and many ups and downs, which I am not at all sorry for, as it made me very early enquire into the "Why's" and serious side of life, became *"nolens volens"* a Mystic.

Well, in my search for Truth, I joined many Brotherhoods and studied deeply and spent of course a lot of money to acquire a first class knowledge. In fact, I worked through most of the branches of Occultism, Philosophies East and West, and Theosophy, and tried as far as I could the whole Yoga system. Well, all of this brought its results, and like you, I am not well off financially. To cut it short, I worked all my life, so to speak, for others instead of saving. That does not sound very wise nor careful, but I do not regret it, for I did get experience, which is after all, everything in life. You see, my attitude is unreservedly plain and blunt. Now my question if you don't mind please.

Why should you make your statement about "Brotherhoods and Lodges on this plane." I must disagree with you. Even Christ was trained by the different Brotherhoods while on this plane. What I have learned up to now is that through all the planes, one is subordinated to the other, because that is The Law. We are all watched and controlled. Nothing is wasted, or goes amiss. Not even Chaos.

I presume you got your statement from your "Guide." Well, to me that does not sound right. Christ said himself he is with us, and instructed disciples to further knowledge and education. He left "living records" behind him. If you are interested, I will lend you some of the works which are kept and printed by our Brotherhood, and I must say that since I joined, I have acquired an immense knowledge which I could not get satisfactorily before. It is the first time I have got real peace.

I will send you pamphlets and show you the whole working of the Order to see for yourself if it is of any assistance to you. You see, I have become very cautious through the many disappointments I have had, and do not blindly believe, but find out for myself and prove the truth.

I hope I have made a new friend and brother. Our Brotherhood is all over the world, and we are directed by the Great White Brotherhood. Prove for yourself whether this is truth or not. I do not persuade you to believe me.

With best wishes and Peace Profound.

COMMENT

In order to follow the gist of the letters, this Brotherhood business must now be explained. My published letter dealt with a certain Occult Brotherhood of the past, having many claimants today to the original title. According to the "inspiration" I received, the *real* brotherhood concerned is mainly existent in another world to this one, and however much it may influence various Groups on the material plane, the fundamental organisation of it is spiritual rather than material.

My correspondent belonged at that time to a Brotherhood which claimed to be the genuine inheritors of that School of Initiation. As you will see, he spent a good deal of time and trouble persuading me to join it and never succeeded in doing so. I could not feel in myself that it was the right one for me, no matter what he or anyone else said. Whatever the higher merits of the Brotherhood may be, I disliked the material presentation of it very much, since it sounded a peculiar and flamboyant note to my English ear. Naturally, my new friend took up the cudgels very strongly for his own side, and we had some splendid disagreements on the subject which we both enjoyed very much.

As he promised, he sent me a considerable quantity of printed leaflets and prospectuses. I criticised these on the grounds that they offended good taste in literature, and seemed to be written for the purpose of "catching customers." Various scales of fees and dues were mentioned, but instead of working through Lodges, the whole thing appeared to be run by correspondence from a foreign country. This did not suit me at all, and I said so in definite terms. That accounts for all the references to the Brotherhood throughout the correspondence.

Now, I have no doubt at all that the Brotherhood in question is an excellent one along its own lines, and especially for the type of people it is meant for. My friend certainly would not have joined it otherwise, and it did him good as he admits himself. That, however, was years ago, and my Friend has now quitted the Brotherhood of which he still speaks well, but appears to make better progress outside of. Each to his own path! There is no Initiate so high that he cannot learn something more. Now for the next letter:

LETTER 3

My Dear Young Brother,

Just had your second letter. Here is a set of pamphlets. Please read all through them and consider carefully.

I have read with great pleasure your letter, and am certainly pleased to notice you think, and take life seriously. I know already you are an older soul in a younger body, which you will clearly understand in the far distant future.

Well, it seems so far you have escaped serious harm. Now I beg of you, whatever you do, don't dabble in Magic. All of which you write, I know very well. Eliphas Levi, with all his learning, made some serious blunders and suffered for it dearly. I am writing this to you to show and prove to you how cautious one has to be in occult matters and affairs. I feel it my duty to warn you, although you are particularly developed, that you must be careful and stick to Mystic work solely, until such time as you are called to assist in magical or higher rites.

By your views, I see that you are certainly a devoted and sincere soul, but of course you are confused in your understanding of it all as yet. Remember, I am comparatively an old man to you, and have travelled far about. To believe is good, but a member of my Brotherhood as to *know* first, and from that knowledge he believes other and higher knowledge. Blind belief is dangerous and even foolish. God has given us the faculties to find out, and to use our "talents" to the best advantage. You remember the parable of Jesus?

Well, all I can advise you is to join the Brotherhood as soon as you can. It will save you a lot of money, trouble, disappointment and hardship. Mind you, were you older, I would not even urge you, but knowing what I went through myself, and what a small fortune I spent in books and studies, and Societies for thirty years, you will understand that I know what I am talking about. Most of the Occult societies and Brotherhoods are known to me, and their activities, but remember, we neither condemn nor argue with any or all of them. Our "Heads" have the traditional Charter and secrets, and as you have deeply taken it to heart, I will lend you a book so that you can see for yourself. I deliberately say to you, do not take my word for it, but see for your own self.

You ask for Truth, well, you shall have it. All forms of religion and philosophies are good and useful, as in all of them is some truth and goodness. That is our attitude. You know what Jesus said to his disciples when they asked him "Why do you tell us one thing and the people another?" — "Unto you it is given, but not unto them, etc." Do you see the necessity for secrecy that we do not cast pearls before swine? All those secret and semi-secret bodies have something, but it is not enough, and at too great a price also, and sometimes connected with danger.

Remember, that with a pure mind and spirit all is well up to a point, but there is the astral danger which in many occult Brotherhoods is forbidden for young, inexperienced people, neophytes and lower grades without guides, on account of the hidden dangers. I know, I had some.

The object that you are on this physical plane is to get experience which you must have. You will know all about it by and by when you understand the Law of Karma, and you will realise why certain Initiates did what they did. Everyone has to go through it. Whether a hundred, a thousand, or a million years, does not matter. It is of nothing in comparison to Eternity.

Remember, it took 40,000,000 years to produce us as we are now in evolution. Think of that!

You appear to know some fragment about our Order, but of merely historical interest. The training, working, and methods are hidden to the outsider. All who are willing, able, and capable of genuine lasting interest are welcome. Many are enthusiastic at first, and drop off afterwards as the path goes on because they are not yet strong enough. Often the apparent least of us are the highest, and the seeming strong and high ones are the lowest.

Do you see the reason for caution and secrecy? An intellectual giant is in far greater danger than the steady, plodding, and hardworking *Soul*. To be humble, means not to be a weak sentimentalist in this world. You have to battle and struggle and fight for a living. That is a force of circumstances, and must be overcome. God does not want you downtrodden, unhappy and miserable. No. Get on, strive for a place, fairly and squarely. Use commonsense, a really not plentiful quality nowadays. Be resourceful, and show the world that you are not a crank or a weakling. As long as you act fairly, then you are entitled to a fair living as a useful citizen. By that you will be an asset to the community, and a pleasure in the eye of God.

Become a leader in service of whatever work you do, and helpful by any little act to anyone who is in need of it. That is the basic principle of Brotherhood. Any good thought or act, simple and practical. You see, I have earned a good bit in my time, but I have not held it up for myself, and I do not regret it. I have learned to be satisfied and believe me, I am really happy. If one loves truth, one lives it to the best of ones ability.

See here. You say that you are looking for a job. Now then. Pray to God, Jesus Christ, or what name you will, to give you the opportunity you seek. Concentrate on that intensely with all your heart and might for a few minutes or less, and then forget about it! An opportunity will come, never mind how or where. When a job comes along that is half way suitable, take it. Don't be nervous or intimidated by anyone, and do the best you can. Do your job conscientiously *to yourself*. God knows better than you do what is good for you. Don't be discouraged or beaten. If you are tired and weary, then take a rest when you can. Forget for a time that you are what you are, and simply concentrate on the job in hand. In your free time, go back to your innermost heart's desire. You will be surprised in a few months time what a change will happen to you and to your surroundings.

You have plenty of time for everything. I know what secret longings are and what enthusiasm means. Curb your impetuosity. Now the time is ten minutes to one a.m., and I cannot finish all I wanted to let you know. See what you can do. More later.

Best wishes and Peace Profound.

P.S.

What you want is ground work. Something to build upon. As a Free-Lance you cannot accomplish a lot. You must realise that you belong to a Whole, and are at present a unit (tiny one by yourself). Later you will understand.

COMMENT

That is, after all, a reasonable approach to Occultism. Sane and commonsense enough in all respects. Just as one would approach any other type of specialised study. It is a singular misfortune for Occultism in general that it attracts so many "cranky" and "eccentric" people. In reality, there is nothing essentially cranky about Occultism at all. In fact, it is very dangerous for any type of unbalanced or abnormal person, and it is only level headed, rational beings who can make any sort of a success at it. As the letter points out, the real purpose of Occultism is and *should* be, to build up and develop human beings to the highest standard they can reach. A good Occultist must be good all through. No one can be good at Occultism and bad in themselves. To be "clever" at Occultism is not the same thing at all, for a clever person can be a bad one as well.

Intellect is a wonderful faculty, but it is two edged, and can be used for evil or good purposes. Goodness of being, and purity of purpose are indeed the very first essentials to seek on the Occult, or any other path. Integrity of character is the only solid and secure foundation upon which to raise the pinnacle of one's Intellect. Moreover, the higher one would develop one's Intelligence, the more important it becomes that the fundamental foundations be deep within oneself, unshakable by adversity, and of a firmness that will endure against Time itself. Upon such foundations, consisting of personal qualities of good and worthy character, one can build the Temple that enshrines one's consciousness according to one's Plan of progress. Goodness, Love, Truth, Kindness, and such Spiritual qualities in us that come direct from God must come *first*. Cleverness, intellectuality, and mental attributes can then be safely developed in the course of time.

That is why I received a caution about "Magic." Properly speaking, Magic is the art of making things happen because we will them to. It is a means of putting Occult laws into practice, and setting Occult forces to work so that they will act as we direct. This idea attracts no end of people to Occultism in the hopes that they will be able to do just whatever they like and get all they want for themselves without having to do very much for it. They believe it to be a sort of Occult "get rich quick" scheme, offering dazzling allurements and rich rewards. At that time, I had very similar thoughts myself, so I can very well understand the feeling. What dreadful mistakes we can make!

Magic, if we like to call it that name, is the actual manipulation of superphysical powers which have a real and positive effect upon not only human beings, but also throughout other kingdoms of nature too. Now you can see why its processes are kept as secret as possible by those "in the know." An evil person can handle those powers and forces with just as much accuracy as a good one. Power is Power, and takes its effect when put into action irrespective of who releases it. Just as we can use the same electricity to kill or cure, heal or hurt, so can we also use Occult forces for good or ill.

Imagine the result if an irresponsible and foolish person were turned loose in a power-house or an arsenal, and told that they could please themselves in any manner they want! Thousands of innocent people might be killed and injured by the idiotic notions of a single fool, who did not even realise what he was doing. Hence, Occult forces, which have greater effects on humanity than all the power houses in the world, are kept guarded by those who have charge of them. A similar idea in a way, to that of international guardianship of the atom-bomb, and for the same reason that humanity could be seriously injured if it got into the wrong hands.

An untrained and unscrupulous "Magician" is just as much a danger as a quite inexperienced but enthusiastic person would be, who attempted to perform a major surgical operation with only the haziest idea of what had to be done, and not caring whether the patient lived or died. Before qualifying as a surgeon, a student has to undergo a complete medical course. Before qualifying as a "magician," an Occult student must put in a similar course of Mystic, or developing, training. That is the correct way.

So far as "Magic" goes, anyone can get hold of all sorts of rituals and practices that have been published many times over, and try out the experiments for themselves if they feel so inclined. That is no guarantee that the experiments will work out as desired at all. Rituals and rites are only channels through which power can flow and take its effect, but unless the power is actually *connected* to rituals and magical practices, there will be no effect worth speaking of. One might just as well wire up a houseful of electric lights and expect them to work without being connected to the "Mains" outside in the street. That makes all the difference. It is this actual connection with sources of Occult power and force which constitutes the "secret" of Magical arts.

Luckily, it is exceptionally difficult for anyone who does not know how, to "make connection" with those forces which are "super-normal" in nature and activity. Nevertheless, it is possible to stumble upon them accidentally, as it were, without realising what one is doing. The chances of such a happening may be remote, but if one "plays around" enough, it may take place and produce results according to circumstances — usually bad ones. This is on the same principle of a school boy mixing up chemicals at random, "just for the fun of it." He may make nothing worse than a nasty smell, or on the other hand, he can quite easily make a cyanide gas which will kill him before he even knows what he has done. Hence the very reasonable warning to steer clear of Magic, or the practical application of Occult powers, until such time as one is fit and trustworthy to use them.

It is so difficult to see all this, or anything like it, in any sort of clarity, when one is wrapped up in the romance and early enthusiasm of ones initial Occult interests. Yet, for the sake of one's future happiness and well being, it is absolutely essential that one should realise the truth. Occultism is *not* a pastime, it is a Power, a Purpose, a Progress, and a Path. It should be treated seriously, and sincerely by whoever wishes to be connected with it. See what the next letter has to say:

LETTER 4

Dear Young Friend and Brother,

I answer quickly, while I have the chance, to relieve any mental or emotional tension which you might have. Steady my dear fellow! You do not clearly understand me. When I suggested you should join our Brotherhood, I meant that you should reap the benefit of its methods and activities. In my experience it does give many more than others here, and in comparison, is far below them in actual expenditure. That is all. I want your best only.

Do you see? Everyone of us has his own Path. You understand quite rightly when you say "all who work in Spirit together for the same Goal, get there." Certainly. I have given you my views regarding our Brotherhood, and have connected myself as regards their activity for Good!!! The very moment I experience anything hindering, or not good, well, it would all be over with them for me. I watch continuously, and if it is in my power with Divine help, I will prevent mischief to anyone. That is the position.

Truth begets truth — and Wisdom. I fear nothing and nobody. I am merely cautious and humble in spirit, as it behoves every aspirant to illumination. Enlightened I am, yes, but not in Light itself, for to be that, I should have to be without blemish or fault. To put it ethically, without sin. I investigate always reverendly, but fearless and firmly. I fear neither God nor the Devil. This is not blasphemy, but I mean it in all sincerity. God, the All-charitable, Omniscient, Omnipresent Love, I need not fear. The other, call him or it what you like, is to be pitied more than feared, for even he is limited, and not eternal, and must eventually work out his own salvation. More truth as I see it.

Please do not judge quickly. Try to understand always. It will save you a lot of perplexity and doubt. You see how I treat you? You will not find any false pride in me. Go on, smile with me. Difference of opinion is good sometimes.

Instinct is the primitive form of guidance. God gave it to all animals and primitive beings, including the humans. You have better than that, my dear brother.

I shall go through your horoscope when I can. Do not attach too much importance to it. From an esoteric point of view, which I hold the only one worth considering, it shows you where you can improve yourself, and your particular strong and weak points. I know Astrology is deeply interesting, and so is Numerology derived from the Cabala, but this is not enough. I find Mysticism as presented by Jesus the Christ the best and safest for us, and in following that, you will learn all else necessary beside. That is the way I have learned. I was enthusiastic about all the different branches too, until I was told psychically and spiritual how to work, and have done so ever since.

>Best wishes, and Peace profound.

COMMENT

This was his answer when I wrote that I did not consider his Brotherhood would be suitable for me, and that I hoped his feelings would not be hurt. It was a broad minded and generous response.

How right he was in mentioning that the byways on the Occult Path are not enough. Some of us spend lifetimes devoted to Astrology, others to the Qabalah, or we try a little of this, that and the other system in turn. At the end of our lives comes the big question: How much good has it all done us? Are we really any the better for it? Has it been worth our while?

No study is absolutely devoid of all results whatever, so that the answer will depend, as they always do, upon the individual. Nevertheless, true Occult development is not, and never will be an intellectual excursion into any single branch of study, but is the balanced and expansive progression of the whole being concerned.

Let me make this clearer. Development, whether Occult or not, is, properly speaking, *growth as a whole*, and is not necessarily confined to any one part of that which is developing. The Occultist therefore says of himself: *I* am developing," and not "such and such a parted of me is making progress." There is a vitally important difference here, because if *he himself* is developing and making progress, then automatically all parts of him are included in the growth. If only a *part* of him is developing, then no matter how well that particular part does, the rest of him may be almost at a standstill.

Supposing, for instance, I wish to develop the muscles of my body. Can I do that by only exercising my right arm? Certainly not. The arm might get splendidly developed *as an arm*, but the rest of the body *as a whole* would be none the better off. Yet, if I properly exercised my whole body, the right arm would develop *anyway*. The same laws apply in this case to Occult as well as physical development. The maxim is: Develop as a whole, and all your parts, which are that whole, will improve; develop only one pat of yourself, and the whole of you will be no better than the single part.

How does one develop as a whole? By "living centrally within oneself, and expanding evenly in all directions around that centre." Pictorially, this would be like a globe getting continually larger by adding to its whole surface. That is the rough idea. In the Occult "centre of you" id the Divine Spark, or Immortal Principle of God in You. It is from this centre that you must grow and perfect your being. Perfect being is *Balanced* being, wherein all the parts that comprise that being, are in continual harmony with each other.

This does not mean that an Occultist must be a "Jack of all trades and Master of none." Not at all. He can be a specialist in any intellectual branch he chooses, providing that his development as a complete being does not suffer thereby. He must not, however, *stop growing in himself*, in order to develop any one especial part. He must continue his whole development *and* that of the part he wills to improve *at the same time*. It can be done.

What is development anyway? It is the process of becoming perfect, and perfection should be our object in Occultism just as in anything else. First and foremost, we must develop and become perfect *as human beings*, for that is what we are *as a whole* at this stage of our evolution. That is the Great Task, or "Magnum Opus" for all of us — to perfect ourselves *as humans!* If we use Occult methods to accomplish this perfection, then we can describe ourselves as Occultists. In all consideration of Occult subjects, one's first thought should be: "How can this make me a better person in myself, and help other people as well?" Otherwise, no Occult study is of my real value to anyone.

Everyone should know the qualities which make up human perfection so far as we can know it. There is certainly no excuse for *not* knowing what they are, unless those in ignorance are really of *very* low mentality and development. As an example of what human development should be, we have Jesus Christ himself, who came to show us what a perfect human being could be like. He did not come to demonstrate his own superiority over everyone else, but to show and teach them how they too, could attain a perfection equal to his own human expression of himself. When his disciples marvelled at him and his powers, he said to them: "These things, and greater than these, shall *you also do*. Everyone *can* be a Master, if they truly *Will* and *work* for that end.

To develop *as a whole*, the aim of perfection *as a human being* must be kept in the centre of one's consciousness all the time, and must underlie all one's active expressions. It is an early danger on the Occult Path, that one forgets or ignores this when particularly fascinated by any one particular branch of Occult study. Supposing one is tremendously attracted to Astrology. Years of study will certainly make a good or *clever* Astrologer, but will that study and intelligence make one a better human being, or in any way nearer to being a Master than before the study was commenced? By itself, it will do no such thing. No amount of pure study will produce a perfect human. It is the development or *actual qualities and powers within oneself* that really counts. Studies are only useful insofar as they may help us to produce and develop the vital qualities of being which alone can make us perfect. That must *never* be forgotten.

All round development of good human qualities is therefore essential in genuine Occultism. This applies to ones faculties, or powers of consciousness too. That is why the advice has been given that one should not attach oneself to any one particular branch of Occult study and exclude all the others. The primary duty of an Occultist is always to *develop himself*, and not any one particular part of him in excess of the others. The *whole* is always more important that the *part*.

Occultism therefore, should never be studied for its own sake alone, or because one is "fascinated" or "attracted" by it. Its sole real value to us, should be for the express purpose of perfecting ourselves for what we really are — human beings! That is what we are here on this earth for, and if Occult means can help us to fulfil this purpose of our life, then we should most assuredly use them to that end, and for that end alone!

Now let us see what is in the next letter:

LETTER 5

My Dear Brother,

I snatch time to give you further information to guide you rightly, for I will see you on the "direct" Path if you will take it. That rests with you my friend.

The position is this. Whatever I said is the unvarnished truth in respect to every reference made. It remains with you to get the correct meaning out of my definite and positive statements. For instance, you thought you saw everything clearly. Well, I will show you that you did not. Please don't get alarmed. Just think slowly and very minutely over it all. I will show you that there is an Art and Science in the method of thinking. By and by you will be gladly surprised at the power of thought and its results. That is the ground work to start with. Get to understand how the Mind works, and what miracles can be achieved with it. But of that later.

I want you to get on, and you shall have Truth and Wisdom as far as, and when, I can give it to you. Now then by Magic, I do not mean more than you realise. It must be understood that you do none of that. What is more, you *could* not, for only High Initiates *can* The minor practices about which you have read, would not even work, for you have not the key nor power, therefore nothing could happen. I mean to warn you, do not try to penetrate or understand that yet, for by so doing, you will attract to yourself that which you cannot discriminate, and is therefore hindering and even harmful.

You feel an inner urge or influence more powerful than you. Well, how do you know the meaning of it? Be careful. You may mean well, believe you are right, feel it correct, and yet later you find it not correct. Afterwards, as you say, you fall, then pluckily get up again and try once more. Quite commendable, but hardly right. Otherwise you would not have fallen. Do you see now? Why fall if it is not necessary? Why not avoid trouble, which is much wiser.

Ceremonies are Symbols in themselves, and are as such employed as a method of working, but you could do the same work without them. Do you understand? Do you know that some people practice Magic unwittingly and unknowingly even, and if you told them so would strongly repudiate it? You were never aware of that?

You must start with preliminary work. That is the position. You have had astral experiences, etc., which proves that you have made a start. You have had glimpses, inspirations and so forth. Very good, but — do you know anything positively to work upon? No. You seek, you drift into this, that, or the other. All is profoundly interesting, dazzling, surprising, wonderful, — but wait, — do you *know* what you are doing? Many people have been misled, suffered great hardships and illusions, until in their dire agony, they were rescued by their prayers. The poor weak souls did what they thought right at the time and got experience. Yes true, but at what a price! They could have had the same knowledge quicker, better, without suffering, had they known. Do you know what their only fault was? Non-knowledge. Ignorance.

God gave each human being a certain amount of free will to work out his own salvation. Fools use it wrongly. Remember the old saying — "Fools rush in where Angels fear to tread," You see, I don't mince matters.

You have everything before you, make use of it. Good use of it. Right thinking, Right acting, Right living, that is the Right way to Right knowledge. Remember all the darkness of the Universe cannot put out one tiny Ray of Light!

Yes, books, the *right* ones, are good friends, and in a way guides, but half of what is printed ought to be destroyed, and the world would be the better for it. My dear Brother, you must get to know your lower self thoroughly. It is written by all Teachers, "Man, Know Thyself!" Very well — do it. Start on it, and watch yourself in relation to everything and everyone, and you will get continual revelations. Be silent.

Self-control is the first step, and the hardest battle. I know. He who can control himself is the one who has the knowledge and ability to control his own life and the lives of others. Remember what Jesus said about the hot, cold and lukewarm? Either be one or the other, rather than the third. Be *something* rather than nothing in particular. Be practical, resolute, fearless. Have faith, but not *blind* faith which is synonymous with superstition and foolishness. You have a certain knowledge. On that build your faith. Hold on to the savings of Christ, and all the other Masters. I will now give you one lesson:

Supposing you want badly to know a certain thing. For example, take any occurrence in daily life such as what time it may be. Don't look at your watch or clock, just ask yourself the question and wait for an answer. *Do not reason.* Do not say "It must be so and so, because of this or that." Just wait calmly and get the answer, the first that comes into your mind. Then, see if you were right. If not, don't bother, but keep on that exercise for a week, and see how often you get it right. You will find out by and by that you get correct results.

Do a few days meditating over it all, and see how it works.

Best wishes and Peace profound.

COMMENT

I certainly was not spared criticism and correction, when and where I needed it! It is a dreadful mistake to imagine any Occult Teacher as a sentimental being oozing with endless sympathy and sentimental soft heartedness. Far from it! No genuine teacher will encourage or condone weaknesses and faults in their pupils, but will point out those faults in a plain and precise manner for the pupil's own good. A teacher will have endless *patience* with the human faults of his pupils, it is true, nevertheless he will always challenge those faults whenever they occur. Remember, an Occult teacher does not criticise his pupils, because he is displeased or angry with them. On the contrary, he does so because he loves them, and only seeks what he knows is best for them. That is the Occult meaning of the text "The Lord chastiseth whom He loveth" (*Proverbs 3:12*). The question of punishment for faults simply does not arise, so far as the teacher is concerned. Pupils are adequately punished by themselves, as a result of their own inattention or disregard of advice given. Having caused my own punishment on many occasions, I can vouch for the truth of this!

In the preceding letter, the power of thought is indicated, and a simple little exercise given as a mental experiment. Now this "power of thought" is a fundamental underlying the whole of Occultism, and unless it is appreciated, one cannot hope to make any real progress on the Occult Path.

THOUGHT IS A POWER WHICH CONTROLS POWERS!!!

If you really want to do yourself an Occult favour, you can print this in large letters and hang it up as a sort of "Text," so that you may be continually reminded of it. Until you begin to know what thought can do, and is capable of, you can have no conception of what Occultism really means. Read and study all you can on the subject of thought, and not a moment of the time you spend that way will ever be wasted.

The power of thought is incalculable *once it can be harnessed and used* by the thinker. It is in this "Harnessing" that Occult secrets come in. In a way, it is similar to the atom bomb. For many years, physical scientists knew the power within the atom to be in existence, but the question was how to *get at* that power and use it as they wanted to. So with thought. It does not take very long to get an appreciable idea of the incredible power that must reside in thought and thinking, but to actually *get at* that power and turn it loose as one Wills, is quite another matter. An Occult and secret matter too, thank Heaven! God help us if such a discovery were made public before humanity became fit to use it properly. The physical atom bomb is bad enough, but if we were to be mentally and spiritually attacked on such a comparative scale, the results would be too appalling to even bear consideration. Quite enough damage can already be done with what limited knowledge we have of thought energy and its direction.

Never make the dreadful mistake of believing that "It doesn't matter what one *thinks*." That is an absolute lie in the first place. It matters far more than the average thinker ever realises. The whole of our present world conditions, and our state of being, is the direct outcome of our thought directed activities. The war was an outcome of thought for that matter. All that Humanity is at present, happens to be result of all that Humanity has ever thought in the past, for thought in *some* form or other, lies directly behind *all* types of activity.

It is the power of thought and thinking, which gives the ability to control and manipulate the Occult and hidden forces "behind" our ordinary material universe. Everyone has this power to a minor degree, capable of producing very limited effects. It is through Occult training and development that one learns how to increase this power steadily and surely, until it is capable of controlling and directing amounts and quantities of force which have effects beyond our present computation. Consider, for instance, the effects which Jesus Christ produced with this rightly called Divine power. He raised the "dead," healed the sick, and did many other types of "miracles." He \frankly told his disciples that they too could make use of this same power, if they were able to develop it in themselves.

Think too, of the tremendous number of "faith-healing" cures that may be met with in our present day. Those are instances of direct "thought power." Countless instances of telepathy can be found in ordinary everyday life. That is thought power too. Wherever one looks, if one seeks to find it, can be discovered effects and manifestations of thought energy. Even a very little experimenting will be sufficient to demonstrate this.

The mental exercise given is a very useful one. Obviously it need not be confined to learning the time by Occult means. It can be used for any intelligent question at all. The reason one should start experimenting with knowledge of the time, or such like simple thing, is so that one can check up on results immediately, and find out how far one is right or wrong. That builds up ones confidence in this developing "sixth sense," as one goes along. This is a most important factor indeed, and we will consider it briefly.

Most people get "flashes of intuition" from time to time, *but*, as the letters point out, how far can one trust them? They may be right, or they may be wrong. Time alone shows. One cannot be absolutely certain, one way or the other, until one learns by experience. The Occultist says very reasonable "Why wait that long, why not *train* and develop these super-physical senses of mine, until I can absolutely rely upon them?" Why not indeed!

So that is what the Occultist does. He trains himself until he develops his consciousness to a level, where those erstwhile "flashes" have no become his normal conscious knowledge. Only by experience and constant practice can this be done. Various exercises, such as have been mentioned are of the greatest help, and should be made full use of. The golden rule is to be able to check results as one makes progress, so that one knows for certain that one is going the right way. It is like consulting a map at regular intervals when one is in strange territory, to make sure one will not get lost.

Learning Occultism is like learning anything else. One has to advance towards distant knowledge from ones present knowledge, and a state of balance must be maintained between the two. With what knowledge you already have, you must reach out and gain the knowledge you require. That is the way it is done, quite logically and reasonably.

It is essential that one should have confidence in ones newly acquired knowledge, and that is the reason it must be checked and re-checked until it can be relied on, and one can really "have faith" in it. That is the sort of faith one needs. There are two sorts of faith. One is based on experience and knowledge, and the other on hope and sincere belief. Both are essential, but the first is to be *worked upon*, and the second is to reach out with, and bring fresh material into, the scope of ones' *working faith* by which one actually "does things." It is this actual *working* faith by which Christ indicated that "Mountains could be moved" (*Matthew 17:20*).

An illustration of this can be given easily enough. "Supposing a perfect stranger came to you and said "Look here, will you lend me a pound? I need it urgently, and will return it in a couple of hours." Would you lend that person the money? In all probability not. You might, of course, be impressed by his appearance, voice, or just "something about him," and take a chance on it. Some few people would. That would be "belief faith," based an a belief that the person was honest and genuine. It *might* be right, and it *could* be wrong. Having no *knowledge* of the person, you could not be sure. Now suppose that a very old friend of yours made the same request. Would you hesitate to lend the money then? No, because you reason very rightly, that they have already returned money borrowed previously, you have known them for years, and have every reason to trust them with far greater sums if necessary. You therefore lend your money on your *working faith* in your own knowledge and experience of the person concerned. That makes all the difference.

Belief *in itself* is not dangerous, but *acting on a belief* which is not based on knowledge may result in harm. "Ignorance of the Law is no excuse" applies very much in Occultism. Just as you can take a does of poison "by mistake" and kill yourself "accidentally," so you can make a mistake in dealing with Occult forces, and through ignorance of what you are doing, case a lot of harm to yourself and others. The maxim here is to always work within the safe limits of your own knowledge, whilst seeking to increase those limits so that your work may be correspondingly enlarged.

It is a primary duty in Occultism to build up a *working faith* within ones consciousness which is capable of being continually increased according to ones experience and development. That is why exercises which can be checked within ones conscious limits are so valuable, and such a useful contribution to ones personal progress.

In particular, it should be mentioned that psychic experiences or "spirit communications" should not be trusted just because they are supernormal happenings, and not backed up by reason and knowledge. There is a foolish tendency to believe in such things, just because they are novel and unusual. Those are no grounds for confidence at all. Quite the reverse in fact. Being "dead" does not make a person any more truthful than when they were "alive." Nor does a psychic experience, however interesting, constitute knowledge *by itself*. We are told in the Scriptures to "*try* (test) the spirts, to see whether they be of God" (*1 John 4:1*), and that is the best advice that can be given. "By their fruits (results) you shall know them" (*Matthew 7:16*).

No true Occultist "leaps in the Dark." He advances steadily by the ever increasing Light of the Illumination which comes from *within* him, enlightening his consciousness wherever he directs it. It is this Inner Light, coming through Knowledge, that can never be put out by all the Darkness in creation.

Here follows the next letter:

LETTER 6

Dear Friend and Brother,

Thank you for the letter and books. I had time to read them, because, like you, I am no without a job.

Regarding Occult work. One must be attuned and fitted for it. Those of us who are ready will be called and chosen. Yes, chose, for we have to be *proved* fit. You see, a lot of us are eager and willing, but that does not mean that we can carry out what is expected, nevertheless, we can all of us assist to the best of our ability.

Now this mandate in Osiris' teaching about taking neither meat nor fish. Although that is perfectly true in every respect, it is not possible for us *yet*. We are not sufficiently developed to maintain a pure diet of Vegetables and Fruits. Our Karma has to be worked off, and not evaded. Living under our climatic, racial, and circumstantial conditions, we must have a strong and healthy body and mind with which to do our work. That is the Almighty's decree. We owe that much to our fellow men and women in the first place, and to God through them. Jesus said so "What you do unto them, you do also unto me, etc." (*Matthew 25:40*) Try to understand this.

A strong healthy body must be kept in a strong healthy mind, and also one must have a strong healthy Soul as well. A perfect triune harmony that must be well balanced before we can have the power of helping other people. You cannot give, if you have nothing in yourself to give away. You cannot help, if you are unable to help yourself. There is a great Truth. "God helps those who helps themselves" must be properly understood. Our attitude must be to *earn* all, not to have it given to us for nothing. Vide the parable of the talents.

Now about the books. Here is an illustration to interest you and for you to bear in mind. Classify readers and students into three categories thus:

No 1. Takes up a book, lecture, or discourse, for information, and being like a sieve, most of it goes completely through and only a very little adheres.

No 2.   Takes in all, irrespective of quantity or quality, and becomes swollen with it all like a sponge.
No 3.   Takes the same amount in quality and quantity, but is a *filter*, retaining what is good and passing out what is useless. These last get the purest and best results.

The same with truth in all its stages, phases and aspects.

Numerology? Yes. Hmm..... There are hundreds of systems, as in Astrology, or any like Art or Science. You read and hear about it all, and what does it produce to you? a maze of information, possibilities, formations, and manifestations. Very true. Which one is correct, or the nearest to Truth? That is the position you are in, is it not so? Well, Pythagoras is the one who left a complete system. He was an Initiate. Do you realise that all that knowledge is purposely veiled, so as not to be abused? Do you know the Cabbalah, from whence numerology has emanated, is a *sacred* science and is not allowed to be broadcast wholesale so that people can use it for a fortune telling stunt? If we were all allowed to know the future, what a confusion it would be fore everyone. Look at the commercialisation there is with it. Look at all the different systems in use already. Can they *all* be right? No. Humanity is weak, and has always struggled for pleasure and ease in its selfishness.

God knows better than you do what is best for you, and is not to be told how to work by you or anyone else. Look at it in that light, and you will see things much better.

Helpers and Masters can only invite anyone to be shown the way. If people refuse to be shown for any reason, then no more persuasion is allowed to be used. That is the mandate.

You know more about me than you are aware of. That may sound queer, but it is so. Now I give you best wishes,

and peace profound.

COMMENT

This aspect of diet must be carefully understood, for it is a more important point than might appear on the surface. The food one consumes has a very definite effect upon ones physical body, and also repercussions upon ones other vehicles too. There is no question at all about a vegetarian diet being the best one for Occult purposes, because that is admittedly so. Whether such a diet is applicable or not to individual beings however, is quite another matter.

Our physical bodies are the inheritors of a meat and flesh eating ancestral custom. This is a very great pity from an Occult viewpoint, yet from another angle it was an essential factor to human development under certain primitive conditions. To ensure the survival of the human race in prehistoric times, it was necessary that human beings should be provided with powerful, gross, and almost animal bodies. No other type of body could have lived under the conditions prevalent in this world at the time. In order to maintain and keep that sort of body going, a flesh diet was the only practicable one, so far as humanity was concerned. Humanity therefore secured physical survival by this means, though it was certainly a deterrent to spiritual progress.

As Mankind developed, the need for animal meat as food became less and less. Meat is the coarsest, heaviest, and most unspiritual type of physical food. With it, one partakes to a certain extent of the animal nature connected with the eaten beast, which in turn fosters and strengthens the purely animal nature of humans who eat such food. Hence the ban on meats by those who sought spiritual development for themselves and their followers.

Purification of the physical body and its animalistic tendencies is absolutely essential in Occult work. A pure soul cannot live in a gross, tainted body, any more than clean water poured into a dirty vessel will *remain* clean. It is a mistake to consider the physical body as unimportant. It is the vehicle of the soul, and should be treated as such, with neither more nor less care than its relative position entitles it to.

A pure vegetarian diet is indisputably the best one for Occult purposes, since the whole "built-up" of body and human consciousness is affected thereby towards a much higher rate of vibration than that of a meat eater. That is absolutely true in principle, but in practice there are individual factors to take into consideration.

Not all human bodies are yet ready to exist purely on a vegetable diet. We still have that animal ancestry behind us which is the Karma to be "paid off," and many of us who attempt to evade it, only do so to the detriment of our physical health. To ruin good physical health through inattention and carelessness, or because of impractical ideals, is definitely wrong and foolish. The physical body must be kept in good working order, and if it still needs meat for this purpose, then meat must be given it for that reason and none other.

It is very true that we should at least eat only the absolute minimum quantity of flesh that will keep our bodies in good working trim for the jobs they have to do. One thing the war has done for me, is to prove to us that we did not need anything like the quantity of meat we once thought we did. In fact, we have been much better without the unnecessary surplus we once overloaded our stomachs and systems with. It should at least be easier for us in the future, to reduce our meat-eating, after such a period of enforced curtailment in the past.

If it is possible for an individual to adopt a purely vegetarian diet, then it is a distinct advantage from an Occult standpoint. Personal circumstances of health, employment, etc., must all be taken into consideration first before such a course is decided on. In any case, a meat diet should not be discontinued at once, but cut down regularly over the course of many months. Even then, if health and physical strength show any signs of failure or weakening, meat must be resumed forthwith. If one can do without meat, then so much the better, but if not, then it is simply a crime against ones physical body and being to enforce a diet having harmful effects upon it. At the present time, vegetarianism is a matter for individual decision and trial. Subsequently, the human race will "grow out of it," but until that time, we must live as our natures direct.

By all means adopt vegetarianism in principle, for it is perfectly correct as an Occult teaching. Practice it too, so far as it lies in your ability without causing unnecessary inconvenience to yourself and other people. Study carefully the effect it has upon yourself, and learn by your commonsense where to draw the line. If it spoils your health, or makes you "faddy" and "fussy," so that other people find you a nuisance, then it is having no good effect on you, and should be drastically modified in your practice of it. Your Occult development will suffer seriously if you force upon yourself anything beyond your means to bear and support. God Himself does not try you beyond the limit of your human endurance, so why should you be more severe to yourself than your own Creator?

It is no part of a genuine Occult life to adopt any peculiarities of diet or custom, which cause inconvenience or annoyance to other people. Apart from any other reason, hostile thought currents directed against oneself from other humans, are a definite hindrance to ones Occult progress. Even if the ability is developed to counteract these currents so that they will not affect one, energy must be used up in such counteraction which would be much better applied for higher purposes. Needless expenditure of energy should always be avoided when possible, and that is one very good reason why Occultists prefer to *remain* "Occult" or hidden from those who are not in sympathy with such matters.

No true Occultist seeks to advertise himself as such to all and sundry. It is not his ambition to *attract* attention of other humans to himself as a student of Occult matters, but to *avoid* such attention as far as he can. He knows perfectly well the power of people's thoughts, and the increased effect they have upon his being, because he has become more sensitive to thought action than an "Ordinary" person. He has no wish to use valuable energy all the time in neutralising a continual stress of unwelcome thought force emanating from unhelpful quarters. Therefore he adopts the best policy dictated by experience, and "lies low and says nuffin!"

Outwardly, the genuine Occultist presents a normal life for the world to see, and only those whom he can absolutely trust are admitted into his confidences. He does this for his own self protection, in addition to the fact that it puts him in a far better position to help those who are really in need of what assistance he has to give. This is actually the antithesis of selfishness, since he only seeks to make his own position the better, so that he will be able to make other people's positions better too. He realises that he must *have* before he can *give*, whether his possessions are physical, mental or spiritual.

This is where selfishness and unselfishness come into the picture. It is a question of human motive, and the result of that motive. A selfish person acquires things and powers in order to have and hold those entirely for the aggrandisement of his own person. An unselfish person acquires the same things and powers, in order to give them away so that everyone else may be the better off for his abilities. That is the whole difference.

Physical things can only be given away once, and the power of giving is immediately lost to the giver, so far as those actual physical things are concerned. Not so with mental or spiritual gifts though. Those with mental and spiritual powers and "possessions," are able to give these way continually to others, and actually be enriched themselves by the giving. Of course, it does depend on those others, how much of those non-physical gifts they are able to *take!* It must also be remembered that no such gifts must ever be *forced* on anyone, only *offered* to whomsoever is in actual need. If there should be any difficulty in understanding this, it should be born in mind that a teacher of any description is able to give his knowledge away continuously to his pupils, yet his own knowledge is enhanced thereby, and is never the slightest whit the less for being given away to as many as can "take it in."

That is the position with the Occultist. If he is on the "Right Hand Path" — of Good, he is able to affect other humans in mental and spiritual ways, which can help them enormously if they are able to receive what they are given. An Occultist is better able to help in this way than anyone else, for the simple reason that he works *consciously* and directs his forces by Intelligence and Will. As his knowledge increases in proportion to his powers, he understands *how* to help people, and that is almost a science by itself. People are best helped, by being assisted to help themselves, and not being made to depend upon the assisting power. Just as a baby must learn to walk by its own efforts, and not remain dependant upon the guiding hands of its parents, so must a human soul learn to act on its own initiative, and not be forever relying upon outside help for all its activities. Largely for this reason, Occult help is generally given in such a way that the person receiving it is unaware of it consciously, and therefore supplements the given help with self-reliant efforts of their own, which they would not exert if they felt that "things were being done for them."

An Occultist realises the Inner Truth of God-in-Humanity, and it is this Divine Principle in Whose service he works. Every single human being bears within themselves a Divine Spark, or Spirit, which is the God-in-You. If you feel inclined to say: "What! Does that mean that in all the vile, degraded, dreadful specimens of so-called humanity which encumber this earth, there is a Divine

Principle?" The answer is unequivocally "Yes, and if you disapprove of that fact, as you have a right to do, what do you propose doing to improve the situation?"

Those degraded ones have the Divine Spark in them as well as you have. That makes the position only the more terrible. If they have deliberately, consciously and wilfully, acted against this Divine Spark within themselves, then they are guilty of what is called the Unforgivable Sin against the Holy Spirit. Luckily, comparatively few people are able to commit that sin, because it must be done consciously, and in full knowledge. The vast majority of evildoers act in ignorance and stupidity, knowing no better than their activities show. They will pay for what they do in the normal course of their development. The truly wicked people are those who know perfectly well what is right and good, then deliberately choose a course of action which they know equally well is evil. These sin against the God-in-Them, and so must suffer for what they do to a correspondingly greater extent than if they acted in ignorance.

It must not be thought that because God is in you, that you are really God. Do not be beguiled into that way of thinking, which certain pseudo-mystical works may lead you to believe. You are a human being, working your way up the scale of evolution towards the Divine Kingdom. As yet, you are essentially *human*, and not even a *perfect* human, though there are certain Divine qualities and attributes within you which you may have a right to call yours. Although you have Divine *potentialities* within you, which you can develop through yourself, you have not yet made these into the *actualities* which they must become in yourself, before you have any real right to call yourself a Divine being.

That is the work ahead of you, to reach the Divine Kingdom, and live in it as your normal existence. The Divine Spark in you shows you the way ahead if you will follow its Light. Ultimately, will come for you the Great Attainment, when you have so perfected yourself, that you will have reached the level of the God-in-You, and That, fusing itself into your perfected being, becomes the Mystic Union which is beyond all human understanding, and you will have reached what has been called "Nirvana" at last.

Do not therefore confuse the Divine Principle in Man, with mankind themselves. That is a grave error. Serve humanity as bearers of the Divine Spark, and give them every possible chance that lies in your power to develop the Light of that Spark within themselves. That is worshipping and serving the Principle of God-in-Them, or as Christ said: "Doing it unto Me" (*Matthew 25:40*). It is also the true meaning of "Loving your neighbour as yourself," when the Love which is the God-in-You, seeks the Love which is the God-in-Them.

This Occult Doctrine of God-in-You can be a dangerous one if misunderstood, and may lead to egomania of a horrible kind. The Roman Emperor Nero was an example of this, and in our own times we have the unspeakable case of Adolph Hitler to show the terrible results which misapplication of this principle can produce. There have been, and are yet, any number of minor cases confined in asylums, all suffering from the delusion that they are God and have Divine Powers. There are less severe degrees of this type of mania in existence, which can yet cause considerable trouble to all concerned. A humorous story serves to illustrate this very well.

It seems that a visitor to a lunatic asylum was interested in the conduct of an inmate, who was striking characteristic poses and muttering to himself. Suspecting what the answer would be, the visitor asked:

> "And who are you, if I may ask the question?"
> "Don't you know?" responded the lunatic in a very offended way, "I am Hitler, the Greatest Dictator of all time. Heil!"
> "Indeed? How very interesting. Who told you that?"
> "Almighty God Himself told me!"

Here a wild looking man leaped to his feet from another part of the room, and bellowed at the top of his voice:

> "You liar! I never told you anything of the kind!"

Quite! It is a very dangerous sort of insanity when men persuade themselves into a belief that they are identical with God.

Truly, God is indeed within Man, but Man is a separate entity from God, being created so, and having the free will to choose whether he would accept the God within him or not. The God within uses no form of compulsion on His created creatures. In a way, You are a part of His Great Experiment, and have your share to perform in ensuring its success. Providing you do the best you can as you go along, you need have neither fears nor worries.

What a Mystic has to do, is to invite the God within him to radiate Divine influence throughout his entire being, so that he may be perfected thereby and eventually attain the Mystic Union. The responsibility for this rests with the Mystic himself. The Divine Principle within him responds entirely in accordance with the way in which the Mystic is able to align himself with the Divine Laws. Think of this Divine Principle within you as a Light, around which you have your being. You have the power to exclude that Light from yourself, screen it so that it is scarcely perceptible to you, put different coloured glasses in front of it so that it gives any tint you please, or you can project all sorts of images like a cinema inside you and around you by means of its illumination. The one thing you can *not* do, is to put it out!

It is absolutely essential that you learn to distinguish between yourself and the God-in-You. Otherwise, when you attempt the mystic practice of doing the Will of God within you, there is every likelihood of self deception being involved, and you will believe that God is directing you in a certain way, whereas in reality you will be directing yourself to do what you wanted to do anyway, and you will think that all the responsibility rests with God. Do not fall into this silly trap, but be honest enough to find out first of all what you want to do personally, then enquire within yourself so far as you can, what the Divine Principle Wills should be done in that particular instance. When you are as certain as you can be about the Divine Will in you, compare the difference of this with your own persona will, and then act accordingly to the best of your judgement and take the responsibility yourself. That is the best way. God did not create you as a negative automaton, but as a responsible being to carry out His Plan by your own free will. The choice is *yours*.

Just as the Divine Principle in you does not compel you to act in accordance with Its Will, so you also *cannot* compel that

Principle to act in accordance with yours. This is a dreadful and tragic mistake made by many people. They believe that they can use the Divine Principle and Its powers within them entirely for their own ends, and to do exactly as they will. This is Black Magic of the worst sort. Worse still, it appears to them and others for a time, that they actually *can* do this, and all sorts of results and phenomena occur which they wrongly ascribe to their own ability and might. They learn too late, that whosoever attempts to grasp the Divine Light within them in order to hold It as a personal possession, shall be indescribably burned by Its Flame. That was the moral in the story of Prometheus. It is also a record throughout history of evildoers and tyrants, wherever they may arise in this world.

Act sensibly therefore in this matter of God-in-You. The action should be reciprocal. As God allows you free will in regard to Himself, answer therefore by allowing His free will in regard to you. Since, with all His Power, He does not force or compel you, do not attempt with your tiny energies to compel or dictate His powers that work through you. You have every right to ask, or request His help, but to dictate your own terms and demand that Divine Power be used this way or that way to suit your own personal purpose, is nothing but stupidity.

It is the purpose of true Occult Mysticism to so train those who follow its Path, that they become enabled to use the powers and forces of the Divine Principle within them in accordance with its Own Laws, and under the direction of Its Intelligence. In this way, those powers are properly delegated to them, and they act, even as the Angels do, in the capacity of Ministers of God. In a way, it is not unlike being promoted as an official in some large Company or other. As a manager or executive, one has the individual authority to act, direct, control, and put schemes into motion on one's own initiative. Yet at the same time, everything one does has to be in the good interests of the Company itself, and because one is its employee. So in true Occultism, "promotion" means that increased responsibility is given to individuals, so that they will be able to administer by their own ability, the Laws and forces of the Great Plan of Creation, in accordance with the design of the Supreme Architect Whose Temple they are engaged on building.

Here is another letter:

LETTER 7

My Dear Brother,

Had your letter, which certainly pleases me. Now to answer you.

Start an unbiased analysis of yourself. Cut feeling out altogether for that purpose, and you will find out a lot. No "ifs," "buts" or "because," etc., just cold discrimination. Spare your emotional feelings. Why spend all that force? See, that is practical Occult economics, or controlling the forces in you!

Now then, your next antagonist — Doubt. While you are in doubt, you are hindered in understanding. You see that, don't you? Well then, why doubt at all? Push doubt from you altogether, and keep an open mind. Neither believe, nor disbelieve, but simply *question* the problem in your mind, and maintain balance by withholding emotion. Stop feeling, or suppress it as much as you can. When you start controlling the forces in you, they are like horses pulling right and left, but you must hold them in rein, and make them go straight. No easy matter! With practice though, it will become more easy to you.

Always aim at all-round development, or else you will go in one direction or another, and have to retrace your steps to cover the essential ground you have missed. Think all this well over. Another thing, you must read more slowly, then you will find it all sinks deeper into your consciousness. Gradually you will notice the difference.

Another point. You are under the impression that it is a disadvantage for you not to know me personally. On the contrary, that is better for your Occult training, since you will not be concerned or occupied with my person at all, but only with what I represent to you. My person should not influence you at all, especially at the commencement of contact. Later on we will meet all in good time. Now smile with me, a sense of humour is essential, what is more, in all its relative aspects. What about a "rough diamond," or a man a bit crude or primitive in his development. He could not see a refined type of humour, but could be helped or guided by a coarse one. All that is necessary even, in Occult work. One cannot tickle an elephant with a feather, but must use something heaver to make him take any notice. See how practical one has to be? Everything and everyone to its or his own vibrations.

Later in time you will often enjoy a joke against yourself, and be full of mirth in a year or so when you reflect on your experience of now. We all do, as we progress.

Best wishes and Peace Profound.

COMMENT

Self-analysis is a valuable instrument in Occult work, providing it is employed correctly. For this reason, it is essential to eliminate all personal emotions and feelings so far as possible during the period of analysis. In that way, one arrives as near the unbiased truth as one can.

That is the Mystical purpose of morning and evening prayers. Each morning, the Mystic makes a conscious dedication of himself to the Divine Power, and determines in a general or particular way how the day ahead may best be used for his own development, and the good of all others within his circle of contact. He asks Divine help in the fulfilment of this purpose. Every night before sleep, the Mystic reviews the day gone by, and studies its events and lessons. He tries to see where he has gone wrong, what he has done right, and what he might have done better. In short, he tries to extract the utmost value out of each day that passes, so that the next day may be so much the better for his improved experience and conscious development. Some Mystical Schools include a midday interval also, as a sort of interim moment during which a kind of auxiliary prayer is made, in order to confirm the morning and re-consecrate the afternoon.

Now this morning and evening period of prayer, meditation, or thought, is of an extremely high Occult value, and an exercise that should be utilised to its fullest extent. All religions recognise its importance, but it rests with the Mystic to use it consciously and knowingly, so that it will have its most potent effect. Used intelligently, it is of the greatest aid to progress on the Mystic Path.

These prayer-purpose-periods are for a higher use than a merely superstitious or force-of-habit calling upon the Deity with a mouth full of words, and a heart devoid of good will or any worthy intention. They are for the practical purpose of raising one's consciousness to a higher than normal level, so that it approaches towards the Divine Inner Principle, and seeks to align workings of that Principle with the workings of one's normal everyday life. After all, the Mystic Attainment of the Supreme Union, is to the end that living in the Divine Principle *will* be a "normal everyday life," so that the Mystic is quite logical in his attempts to establish a conscious basis in himself whereby the Divine and Human Principles within him may be linked.

It is essential, in the use of these periods as an Occult and Mystical exercise, to consider the factor of rhythmic and regular repetition, without which, they will have very little effect. Rhythm, in fact, is their keynote, and the Laws of Rhythm, or Vibration, are Occult fundamentals of the greatest importance. That is the purpose of having morning, afternoon (midday) and evening periods, which will form a powerful vibratory sequence throughout the whole life and being of the practitioner. Since vibrations are the cyclic in action, let us consider for a moment a single cycle of this periodic practice.

It commences in the morning, when, after the night's period of rest, all the faculties associated with material existence are refreshed and renewed. The earth's forces, and the Magneto-electric atmosphere are also newly active as well, so that harmony is established with Nature itself. This is the moment when the Mystic dedicates all the forces of which he is a symposium, to the Divine Inner Principle in Whose service he seems to spend the day. In a sense, it is somewhat like the essential moment of calculation and concentration before one makes a high dive into a swimming pool, so we can use this as an analogy. Having made his preparation, the Mystic then takes the plunge deeply into the ordinary affairs of his daily life.

The midday period is similar to "coming up for air" in order to find out how ones progress under water has gone along, and where it has taken one. Being reassured on this point, one then makes what corrections may be necessary, and then plunges again during the afternoon. After midday too, the earth's natural forces "swing over" as it were, into the diminishing aspect of their strength, so that the Mystic works in conjunction with Nature again.

In the evening, when the day's activities are over, and the other side of it has been reached, the Mystic climbs out of its river of Life, and sits down awhile on the firm ground of his own Inner being, to think about it all. He reviews his own actions and experiences, those of the other people he has encountered, and tries to see them all in the light of their real values to each other and to himself. To do this, he has to adopt as impersonal an attitude as possible, so that his judgement will not be overclouded by his own emotions and feelings, which would otherwise give a one-sided and personal bias to the whole picture. Still acting in unison with Nature during the evening, the Mystic gathers up his forces within himself and epitomises his expenditure of them during the day.

The remainder of the cycle is completed during the night through the higher stages of consciousness in which the Mystic works whilst his physical body lies asleep, and carries through until the following morning, when it recommences on the physical plane of existence.

In this way, it is possible to periodically align ones consciousness with ones normal and supernormal existence, so that each has a bearing on each other within ones actual experience. That is why this practice is of such high Occult value if used intelligently. The important point to bear in mind is that it must be *regularly* used, and not merely resorted to intermittently, even though that is better than not at all. The reason for regularity can best be understood by an analogy, which everyone can convince themselves of by practical demonstration if necessary.

The analogy is the well-known pendulum demonstration showing the cumulative action of applied energy. A heavy pendulum is hung at rest, and tapped lightly and rhythmically with a pencil, or such light article. At first, no physical effect is perceptible, but after a while, slight movement can be detected, and as the demonstrator goes on tapping it, using just the same amount of trivial energy every time, and hitting the thing precisely at the moment when it begins to swing in the opposite direction, the pendulum gathers momentum with every swing and becomes and more powerful in action.

By using regular periods of prayer, meditation, thought direction, concentration, or what form of conscious energy you will, you put into action the spiritual counterpart of this physical law, and feel the results of it in your own being. If you choose morning, midday and evening as the times for these periods, you will have the added advantage of acting in harmony with the great etheric forces of the world itself, which underlie all purely physical phenomena. These forces are infinitely more powerful than you are, and it is just as well to get all the benefit you can from their activity.

The whole idea is simple enough really, for it is just tackling the problem of your Occult development in a sensible way, and doing little by little what you have not the power to do all at once. A glance back at the pendulum will show this, because if it were hit only once with all the energy of countless little taps, it would swing just as violently from that single blow as it would from an accumulation of all the little ones spread over a much longer period. It is the same with spiritual or Occult development. If you could make one terrific effort, you could get the same effect as by making a tremendous amount of small ones. This however, is not practical, because in the first place it is far beyond the power of any normal human being, and also the violence of its application could have dangerous repercussions. Little by little is the best way to develop and work up any power, Occult or otherwise. Then it becomes increasingly greater with every rhythmic repetition, and also becomes a permanency and a reliable attribute, instead of an intermittent and undependable power.

For this reason, if you intend commencing this practice as a means of development, follow its own laws and place a deliberate limitation upon your first attempts at using it. There is no sense at all in starting off with a tremendous splash, then slowing down and abandoning the practice altogether. It is precisely the opposite effect which is required. Do not commence with any long prayers, or sustained efforts of thought, which are not usual for you. A few seconds, and a brief thought will be quite enough to begin with until such time as the habit is definitely formed, and you can be quite sure that it can be relied on as a regular and dependable habit. When this is certain, which may take days, weeks, or even months, you can then extend and enlarge the periods as you feel necessary.

At first then, a simple thought such as "God help me to do my best today" in the morning, "I could have done better this morning, but I'll try harder this afternoon" at midday, "The experience I have had today can be used to improve me tomorrow" at night, will be sufficient to start with. The important thing is that this be done *consciously* and intentionally. It has a much greater effect if put into prayer form, since then your spiritual aspect will be called into conscious activity as well. First, however, make the habit. When made, you can build upon it to suit your own requirements.

It must not be forgotten that the aim of these periods is to develop a higher than normal consciousness and bring it to bear upon your ordinary state of mind and being, so that this too is given an impetus toward the higher levels. A few words of explanation are needed here to make this more clearly understood.

The normal, working level of your consciousness is that which you usually live in, and which is closely associated with your active, mundane life. You can reach much higher levels than that, but in order to do so, you must stop all normal activity and thought, directing your whole attention and concentration towards the level you intend to reach. You should easily see this, when you consider that you cannot play some vigorous game and study mathematics, or anything else, at the same time. When reaching out to a higher level of consciousness than normal, and therefore a new level so far as you are concerned, all your activities and forces must be turned in that one direction.

You are therefore faced with this problem. While functioning in a higher state of consciousness, you cannot live your normal active life, and while you are acting and living normally, you cannot exercise your higher conscious faculties at the same time. How then are you to raise the level of your normal thought and living? The answer is by means of these periodic exercises we have been considering. Each time they are performed, the working level of your consciousness is raised a fraction higher than before, and so you will make progress by a continual series of easy stages. That is the Occult way.

It is of great importance then, that while performing these periodic practices, you give your whole activity towards them. It is of little value for instance, if you try to pray or concentrate while you are struggling with your shoe laces in the morning, even though that is better than not at all. Remain absolutely still physically, exclude all ordinary thoughts as far as you possibly can, and then make one real effort to reach up as high as you can within your spiritual perception and formulate your conscious prayer or thought, when you feel that you have reached that state. This need only take you a minute, or maybe less. It is the sincerity, intensity, and reality of your thoughts and prayers which really counts. Ten seconds of genuine thought or prayer are worth immeasurably more than hours and hours of uttered words, which have neither meaning nor value to you. What is more, those ten seconds of sincerity would have an infinitely greater effect on you, than all the hours of lip service you could waste. One of the most remarkable effects of prayer I ever knew of, came to a man who had "never bothered," as he said, to pray before, and being in the depths of utter despair, uttered only three words from the very foundation of his soul: "God help me." Nothing more than that in actual words, but the effect they produced would be unbelievable top anyone not knowing the man personally, therefore I shall not tell his story, beyond saying that his whole life changed from misery to happiness during the course of a few months following his prayer. It is intensity and depth of consciousness which produces results. Remember the lines from Hamlet:

"My words fly up. My thoughts remain below.
Words without thoughts, never to Heaven go."

Once the Occult significance of these rhythmical and reiterated periods of higher-consciousness working is realised (which only practical experience can teach), you will find that the fundamental principle can be applied to any specific conscious process you may intend to develop. Just as constant dropping of water will eventually wear away a stone, so will many small efforts of consciousness directed towards the same objective each time, ultimately succeed in having a proportionate effect upon the objective aimed at.

One point about self analysis. It is an excellent practice if used as a separate process of consciousness, but it can be a hindrance if allowed to interfere with normal working-level activity. This happens when one tries to keep a sort of analytical eye on all ones actions whilst engaged upon their performance. The result of this is a split consciousness, and one tries to think from both angels at once. This simply "sets on state of consciousness on to the other," like a pair of antagonists, and the outcome is that neither does any real work worth mentioning, because each is so "taken up with" the other, that there is little energy to spare for anything else. The answer to this is to stay in one state of consciousness at a time. Analyse or act according to your own will, but do not attempt both together. Make your calm analytical decisions first, then give yourself over to the activity decided upon, and concentrate upon that alone whilst doing it. When finished, or during an interim, analyse again and make what corrections or improvements may be necessary. Alternate the two states of consciousness but do not try to achieve them simultaneously. Remember the maxim "What thou hast to do, do with all thy might!" i.e. with *all* your undivided conscious attention.

Another very important question was raised in the last letter, which deserves consideration here — a sense of humour. It is not out of place to connect this with Occultism at all. To the contrary, without it there is little hope of making any real spiritual progress, for it is essentially a gift of the spirit, and lightens the hearts and natures of mankind whenever it touches them.

Like other faculties, it can be perverted and used in the wrong way, as for instance, a malicious sense of glee over the distress of discomfiture of some disliked person, or a "fiendish delight" in tormenting or worrying other beings. It is not this undesirable side of it however, that the true Occultist seeks to cultivate. He associates humour with that pure joy and happiness which comes spontaneously with an harmonious state of well-being, and a kindly sense of understanding with his fellow creatures.

A student of Occultism should understand the important difference between laughing *with* people and laughing *at* them. An undeveloped person laughs *at* others, because, being mostly confined within the narrow limits of his own personality, he has not yet learned how to share other states of consciousness than his own cramped one. Therefore he has to remain as it were shut up inside his personal prison, directing the shafts of his consciousness through the small windows at whatever may be exposed to his view. The deliberately expanded consciousness of an Occultist or Mystic, works far beyond such limits, since it is able to share itself with that of other souls. Such a consciousness does not laugh at faults or distresses in others, since it feels with them, and appreciates their viewpoint from its own angle. It can, and does laugh with their gaiety and happiness, because their joy becomes its own as well. It works on the principle that although a sorrow shared may be a sorrow halved, a joy shared is a joy doubled.

Humour is a saving grace which rescues the true Occultist from many a pitfall. It saves him from pomposity, false pride, self-importance, and a host of personal faults which arise from the root-evil of egotism. In making him agreeable to others, it brings him the value of their kindly thoughts and sympathies. Therefore he learns to cultivate it and apply it to his life and the lives of others around him, so that the happiness of all may be enhanced thereby. Blessed indeed are they who have learned to find the humour, and consequently the pleasure in whatsoever they encounter.

I once saw the practical working of this principle in a monastery. The monks were easily the most continually happy people I have ever met as a community, yet their secret was simple enough. They had learned how to find pleasure and happiness *within themselves and each other*. Because that Inner happiness was always there, very small and simple external happenings were sufficient to bring it out of them in the form of laughter and smiles. They smiled cheerfully on the slightest occasion. A small and trivial slip of my tongue in their native language, became the joke of the monastery for several days. In fact, they found some reason to be happy wherever they possibly could. They were wise with the wisdom of deep spiritual experience.

Those monks demonstrated the truth of the Occult precept that happiness is essentially an *interior* quality of being. It is commonly thought that external happenings, which have an association with some kind of pleasure, are the cause of human happiness. This is not really so at all. External happenings or material things, can be used to evoke and give a physical framework to happiness, which is already in the human heart and soul, and that is the best they will do. If happiness is there, *inside you*, in the first place, then you can call it forth into whatever material circumstances are available to suit your purpose. If you are miserable inside yourself because of your own disordered condition of mind and soul, then nothing which this earth has to offer will make you happy by its own powers, no matter what you may think to the contrary.

Happiness and joy are inseparable from humour, and since the ideal condition of perfect balance and harmony of being means that both joy and happiness are experience, it follows that humour is an essential element for the attainment of any stage of perfection. This is just as true in Occultism as for other Paths of progress. The earlier Mystery Schools knew this perfectly well, and used to celebrate certain of their Rites with laughter and happy joy as a form of devotion. So should it be. When the world learns again how to approach God with happiness and laughter, then the troubles of mankind will rapidly diminish. False solemnity and superstitious self-consciousness disguised as reverence, are no approaches to the Divine Principle. The Mystic way is through open-hearted sincerity and happiness, reaching out towards an All-encompassing Love, which, being true Happiness in Itself, is also the fount of everlasting Joy —and Humour!

Now let us see what pointers can be obtained from the next letter.

LETTER 8

My dear Friend and Brother,

Had your letter today. I knew that you had been thinking about me, and wondering why I had not written before now, but I have been having a most unsettled time of it. Still, everything is part and parcel of experience, and the essential thing is to remain balanced, level-headed, and stout hearted. Whatever comes to you, do the best you can. Life may be sometimes unpleasant and hard, but it is necessary, and widens ones tolerance and understanding.

We cannot always do what we want to, and must submit ourselves to superior knowledge and power. Man chooses and God disposes. Wriggle and plan as we will, we have only a certain amount of free will after all. One thing I must tell you. *Do not worry!* One *can* help "not worrying." It simply has to be checked. Worry is Fear, and that is not only useless waste of energy, but is a magnetically destructive force, very powerfully so, and upsets ones whole balance. Without that balance, nothing can be achieved.

Now I tell you, do not try to force things. Keep your desires more in control, and let your attitude towards Occult development be a persistently steady will to develop and concentrate your inner faculties by way of prayer, and leave it to the Divine Will. Send out your own will with the intention of joining it to the Divine Will, and patiently rely without doubt or hesitation for all to come right.

Self conquest is always the hardest battle. How can you know such phases of life as disappointment, depression, agony of mind, soul and body, if you have not been through such things themselves? How can you cope with such things if you do not know about them? The hard thing is to endure all, and have patience. I know. Through the want of that, I lost many points in my time. I tell you all this so that you shall get the benefit of my mistakes.

Remember, Mysticism comes before Magic, and in fact incorporates it. First and foremost therefore, get Mystic training, the other will come by itself as a matter of course, no matter what you may have hard to the contrary.

Now I will tell you what I do if a thought current comes to me that I do not want. I pull myself up, and say mentally: "Stop! This is wrong, and I will not have it so." That soon puts a stop to all nonsense. If not, then I make a call for help and strength to God, and make a grim resolve to be strong and overcome the difficulty. Is it not natural that you should get difficult thought currents and phases?

Never mind about old incarnations. It is NOW which concerns you. Don't waste time bothering about what you were in the past. The point is what you are now, and to get fresh experience. Be careful about your "Messages," remember, one can be fooled by "Spirits," just as well as by humans. I know what I am talking about. I have been fooled in my time too. You know the behaviour of a wireless set? A clairvoyant is just the same. Sometimes one gets very indistinct results.

Keep a calm steady attitude of mind. Then your thoughts will be powerful. I told you before, how to send messages to the Cosmic, and put the message out of your conscious mind. That is the way to release the thought. Now best wishes, and keep up a cheerful heart.

Yours Fraternally,

COMMENT

How correct the writer was in saying "Do not worry!" No true Occultist dares to let himself be overcome by this really destructive force. It is a most deadly enemy of progress, as I can personally testify from my own experience. Every effort must be made to understand its nature, and how to deal with it when it arises.

Worry is a condition of consciousness in any person who is faced with some problem or circumstance in connection with which that person feels uncertainty, doubt fear, and a sense of inferiority so far as the circumstance or problem is concerned. It is a result of the feeling that we have not the personal power to tackle that problem, or whatever it may be, and that there is a strong possibility of failure looming ahead of us, or some unpleasant fate which we cannot very well avoid. It is a lack of confidence in ourselves, lack of trust in God, and an unbalancing of our consciousness. Altogether, it is a very unpleasant and unhappy state to be in.

Real concentration is impossible when in a state of worry, and, of course, any sort of Occult work is altogether out of the question when in that condition. Hence the Occultist avoids it for what it really is, a pestilential psychic disease which can be both prevented and cured, by the application of both common sense and determined will.

In a condition of worry, one actually loses ones state of mental and psychic equilibrium to say nothing of the spiritual side of ones being. The etheric, or "magnetic" currents, which should flow and circulate with regularity through the channels of ones superphysical vehicles, are thrown out of harmony, and fluctuate wildly around, causing all sorts of psychic weaknesses and disorders in the process. Instead of working properly, the mind also becomes disjointed and haphazard in its operation, in which state it is naturally quite unreliable. If the condition of worry continues for any longish period of earth-time, the physical nervous system and even the functions of the human body become affected also, and nervous, digestive, and other forms of physical disorders will occur. Worry upsets balance in all planes of ones existence.

Concurrent with worry, is a tremendous wastage of forces, and a "running-down" of human energies. A worried person uses up energy at a great rate, and produces no other effect with it than to upset his own being, since it is all going to waste "inside him." An apt analogy would be the short-circuiting of an electrical cell, which has the effect of making that cell turn loose its whole energy inside itself to accomplish nothing else than its own destruction. So in the case of worry. Ones forces are turned loose against each other to the detriment of them all, and oneself as a natural consequence.

So much for the rough description of worry, now what about its fundamental cause? Do not look for that in any external circumstances, no matter how fearful their nature, since those are the occasions only which serve the purpose of frameworks, into which can be projected the *internal* condition of worry which arises in the human being concerned. That is to say, it is not external conditions in themselves which have any especial power to worry us, but we permit worry to arise within us on account of our connection with those conditions or circumstances. It is *You* who do everything on account of the "things," and the remedy lies in your own hands.

The fundamental cause of worry is your own abdication of the central Inner Throne, from whence you should administer and rule the forces and energies within you which should be under your control. This statement needs amplification to make it clearer, for it must be fully understood and appreciated to the full of its Occult meaning.

You are a being living in a combination of vehicles, physical, etheric, mental, spiritual, etc., and your task is to direct the progress of those vehicles along the course of the Path you follow. In a balanced and harmonious state, you are as it were enthroned in the centre of all your parts, and should govern from that point the powers and forces which keep your vehicles in "running order." The word "vehicle" is a very apt one, for that is the function to yourself of your various bodies and the powers appertaining to them. You are in the position of a driver in respect to them, and should be normally in the "driver's seat" with all the controls ready to your hand.

Now we will suppose that you are driving along the Path of your conscious life, and some obstacle or difficulty comes into your view. If you are a good driver, you will steer your vehicle so as to avoid, or so as to guide yourself in relation to the impedance ahead, that you will suffer no check or hindrance to your progress. It depends upon shill, self-confidence, judgement, and the use of your faculties in manoeuvring your car. There are innumerable obstacles in life, calling for different treatment, various sorts of control, and a variety of ways of handling, all of which have to be learned, practiced, and perfected. Since most of us are "learner drivers" so far as our higher vehicles are concerned, the element of worry comes in very strongly to hinder our progress when we are not quite certain of our way ahead, and unsure of how to control our vehicles to our best advantage.

For instance, we see danger ahead which is in line with our present course. A state of worry is analogous to a driver who under such circumstances loses all confidence in himself and his car, and frantically fiddles with every control in sight, blindly hoping that something will happen to avert the calamity. Perhaps he will be lucky, but even in that case he will be so nervously shaken, that his driving will be very poor for some time to come.

When in a state of worry, you do much the same thing. You perceive something unpleasant or difficult approaching you, and because it is out of your control to alter its course, you get "panicky" and uncertain about your own controls, or your ability to get out of the way. The more you worry, the worse you get, and the more erratic and wild the course of your vehicle, because your lack of control and attention is letting all its powers run to ruin. You may meet the fate you were afraid of, or you may avoid it. If you encounter it, you could probably have saved yourself by calm control, and if you miss it, there was no necessity to worry in any case, so that worry is altogether useless.

Worry is associated with these main factors. Fear based on uncertainty; anticipation of being involved in something unpleasant; a lack of working faith in yourself, and your own powers which prevents your use of those powers; and a belief in your own inability to control your own situation in respect of whatever is the object (or outside) in connection with which you are worrying. All these conditions and their allied results, produce the outcome which has already been mentioned.

One important point which leaps to the eye, is that worry is nearly always associated with the *future*. Even when you worry about past events, your essential reason for doing so, is because of the effects which you fear those may have on your future. If you were absolutely certain and positive beyond all doubt that you could not possibly escape a coming evil in any way whatever, you would then cease to worry about it. There is therefore a certain element of hope behind worry, but being unsupported by faith and confidence, it is of extremely little value. Desire is also present (in the shape of a desire to avoid the trouble feared), but not having the support of Will, is insufficient by itself to have any great effect. To sum things up, a worried state of being is one in which the higher faculties are inoperative, and the lower faculties are allowed to run wild. It must be clearly understood that worry, like anything else, is a matter of degrees, and that we have been considering it from a point of view of its essential nature. Worry can be a condition varying from a trifle, to a very serious state, depending on the degree, duration, and intensity of it. From the Occult point of view, it is dangerous in any degree, and the Occultist takes steps accordingly to prevent it happening within himself as far as he possibly can.

How does he do this? Largely by the commonsense realisation that worry deprives him of the very thing which enables him to deal successfully with its occasions, namely the control of his forces and the concentration of his powers. Worry is the reverse of concentration, it is dissipation. Concentration is bringing forces and powers to bear upon a focus so that their result will be a most effective one. Dissipation is the wastage of forces in many directions, so that their effects are of negligible importance anywhere. This last point precisely what the Occultist trains himself to avoid, by means of his conscious Will.

If you allow yourself to worry about any difficulty of danger, you seriously hinder the operation of the very forces in yourself which could enable you to cope with it to your best advantage. That is why it is so extremely foolish to worry. By so doing, you will put yourself in an analogical position to someone who might be in a locked room which was on fire, and who wildly threw the key out of the window, hoping someone would find it and release him from outside, instead of calmly unlocking the door from within and simply walking out of the danger. By letting yourself get into a worried condition, you automatically damage your best means of tackling whatever it may be that you are worrying about.

An Occultist *dare* not allow himself to worry, because he knows that whatever injuries he might receive from a threatened danger, there is no reason to inflict the injuries upon his own being which worry can cause. The worse the threat, the more need for him *not* to worry about it, since he must have all his faculties working in perfect order and with the greatest effect, so that he may be fully equipped to deal with the situation with the maximum of good results to himself and others concerned. Come what may, he must remain balanced nd in control of his forces. If the situation really does show distinct signs of being beyond his own ability to tackle, then he still does not worry, but sends out a call for help to the Higher Intelligences. That call will always be answered, and be it noted here that such help is the more readily received, because of the already existing state of balance and control in the person calling for assistance.

Seeing that ignorance is such a strong fundamental of worry, the Occultist does all he can to improve his knowledge in every possible way, thus lessening his danger to the extent of his wisdom. He practices balance and poise within himself, so that he may remain unshakable by external influences. He learns by practice how to control his emotions and mental currents, so that these shall not betray him. By practice again, he builds up his working faith and confidence in himself, his own ability and powers, and above all in the Divine Power and the Great Ones who are in direct support of him.

To be told "don't worry," therefore, does not mean that nothing exists which one can worry about if one so chooses. It means that you *can* worry, but you *musn't* do so. When an occasion arises over which you might worry, or are tempted to do so, try tackling it in the Occult way for a change, and see how it works. Such occasions are not fit moments to "lose your grip on yourself" and dither with apprehensive uncertainty. The very *worst* time to indulge in such stupidity in fact. That is when your mind must be at its clearest, your powers at their greatest, and everything in your whole nature at its very best in order to get yourself through the difficulty by safely, or at worst, with the least possible trouble.

"Don't worry" does not mean to simply sit back and let things take their course no matter what happens. That is a "don't care" attitude, which is also a stupid one. The right thing to do instead of worrying, is to call up your reserves of thought, energy, power, intelligence, and all the strength you can muster, and apply these in the best way you can, so that they will deliver you from whatever might otherwise worry you. If those are not enough, then have no false pride about the matter, but ask for help by means of prayer.

If you ever feel curious on the subject of whether God will hear your prayers or not, you may rest assured on that point for one especial reason. Never forget that since God is Omnipresent, he is of necessity *WITHIN YOU*. His consciousness is linked with yours through its own peculiar channels. Therefore if *you* can hear your own prayer, so also can *He*. Surely that is logical and plain enough. As before said, the deeper you can reach within yourself towards that Divine Principle, the better will the prayer be heard, and the greater the response.

Do everything you can to avoid worry therefore, because it is a state of disease which will most seriously retard your progress in every part of your being. It is *not* easy to conquer worry, and there would be no sense in pretending otherwise. Nevertheless it must be conquered sooner or later if you mean to develop yourself, and the earlier it is overcome, the sooner you will be able to devote yourself to more interesting matters.

Before leaving the subject of worry, here is an illustration from my own experience which may be helpful, and throw a side light which may serve to illuminate the details somewhat more clearly.

At a certain period of my life I was living under a constant threat of danger. That is nothing very unusual in these times, but the intensity and duration of it wore down my resistance to a point where I most foolishly and unnecessarily allowed myself to get into a dreadful condition of worry and strain. This went on and on for days and nights until it seemed that the final climax was reached, and I could see nothing but horror and catastrophe ahead. Imagine my amazement, when I became slowly aware that the *real* "I" was not worried or perturbed at all!

What literally happened, was that I became conscious in a state of being which was higher than that in use on this physical plane. While in that state of consciousness, I realised that in the true sense of "Me," I was something quite apart and distinct from all the terrible conditions which my lesser vehicles and states of conscious being were undergoing. It was an extraordinary experience which I found too difficult to understand at the time, because I was trying to function on both planes at once. I was conscious of myself as an observer of what went on within me, and watched all the emotional disturbances of fear and worry without feeling affected by them. If this should sound far-fetched, bear in mind that it is possible to watch a surgeon operating on ones own anaesthetised limbs without actually feeling the slightest physical pain.

As it was, I made no effort from this higher plane of consciousness to interfere with what went on inside my worried parts of being. To tell the truth, I was too fascinated at the novelty of the experience to do other than watch, and try to make out what it all meant. It puzzled me how I could possibly suffer agonies of fear and worry, and yet not feel them at all at the same time. Both parts of my being were sentient, yet one was going through hell, and the other was calmly watching it without the slightest disturbance. It took quite a long time before I realised what was actually happening. My knowledge came somewhat too late to save me from damage which had already occurred, but it has been of inestimable help since, and I do not grudge the price I paid for it, even though I could have had it far more cheaply another way.

If you can get to realise the essential difference between "*YOU*" and the state in which "*YOU*" live, then you will make a great advance of consciousness. These are two distinct and separate principles altogether, even though existing in conjunction with each other. Thus, it is no correct from an Occult viewpoint to say "I am worried" or for that matter "I am" anything else. Instead of that, accustom yourself to thinking and saying "I am living in a *state* or *condition* of such and such." That makes all the difference, and once you reached a realisation of it, then you can begin to exert the authority of the "I" which is your Self, over the various states of being and consciousness wherein that "I" lives. It is more than half the cause of worry and such similar states, that the difference between *YOU* and what you experience owing to your state of being is not perceived, and therefore you do not realise your own power to affect those state of being in accordance with your Will.

Now here is a little "Occult trick" which I have found most useful in emergency, when something suddenly turns up which appears likely to be an occasion of annoyance or worry. It is simply to take a dozen or so very deep, slow, regular breaths in conjunction with the following mental exercise.

During the inbreath, mentally direct that allo the vital energy of the indrawn air, or "Prana" as the Yogis call it, be concentrated towards that point of your body which lies just underneath where the ribs join together in the front and centre of your torso. You can easily recognise it, because that is where you get a "funny feeling" when you get a nervous shock which "upsets" you. Imagine as you breathe in, that power is rushing in to you and all going to that nervous plexus in order to strengthen it and calm its disturbed condition. Visualise this action so far as you can.

When you breathe out, visualise this concentrated psychic energy as streaming out of you, and as it were, condensing to the extent of a few feet all round you, so that it forms a protective atmosphere of force around your person, through which no disturbing influence can break. By doing this, you will actually accomplish what you have visualised, and build up a field of "magnetic" power around yourself in which you can act with greatly increased efficiency and protection. Naturally, the whole of this practice must be done confidently and resolutely, or it will not work properly. A point to note, is that its effect is not of any long duration, and so, when you feel the effect "wearing off," you will have to repeat it again if necessary. This really is a very welcome help in trouble, and the initial results are apt to be most pleasantly surprising. It will not produce absolute miracles, nor may it have a *completely* calming and balancing effect at first, yet nevertheless it will certainly have sufficient result to prove its value to you, and the development and improvement of this practice is up to yourself.

Now for a different note on a subject of the last letter — reincarnation. It is quite true, as the writer says, that it is of no especial help during early Occult training to try and remember ones previous lives. If memories come through by themselves, well, let them do so, and attach no special importance to them. If not, then make no special attempt to unearth them from the depths of your being.

A favourite question, and quite a justified one, is "If I have lived before, then why don't I remember it?" The answer is quite simple. It is because you are trying to remember with the wrong part of your consciousness for such a purpose. Your *ordinary* conscious memory, which is bound up with this one earth life of yours, knows nothing of what happened to you in any other state of being. How can it, since it is only a record of what has occurred in your experience since this physical birth? The part of your consciousness which *does* remember your previous lives, lies very, very deep within you, and is not normally in direct contact with your ordinary senses. Hence the apparent lack of memory.

The fact that you do not remember previous lives while living in your normal consciousness, is no disadvantage to you at all. The value of the lessons you have learned before, comes to you just the same in the form of effects on your character and being. To understand this, consider the case of someone who has been severely burned when a very small child. In later years, that person would have a horror of fire, while having no conscious memory of the original incident at all. So with reincarnation. You feel the effects of your past lives in many subtle ways, while you cannot call to your normal consciousness the original experiences which produced those effects in you.

It is better that way. Odd flashes of memory which connect with previous lives are apt to be very confusing, and a definite hindrance to the correct living of this one. You cannot alter what you *have* been, but by giving your whole attention to the way you live *NOW*, you can alter your whole future for the better. Even though you may realise that you do reincarnate, the thing to do is to live as though you only had this one life in which to perfect yourself. That will speed your progress tremendously. It is stupid to think "Never mind, I'll do it in my next life." That is a weakness to be avoided with caution. Why slow down and unnecessarily procrastinate your progress? It is obviously true that certain things will unavoidably be held over till "next time," but that is no excuse for not making the best progress you can in this life, without unduly "forcing the pace."

Instead of bothering about what you *were* and *did*, concern yourself directly with what you *are* and *do*. That is good, practical Occult advice. Rest assured that nothing you ever did or were is irrevocably forgotten, and when you have advanced in consciousness to a sufficiently high point, everything will "come back to you" as a natural consequence. If you get odd "flashes," simply maintain an open minded interest towards them, but do not let them influence you to any absurdities of egotism. Memory of all types is a most fallible faculty, as you can realise when trying to recall past events in this life. For example, in connection with reincarnation, you might have a distinct "flash" of an ancient Egyptian Temple. The inherent vanity attached to your normal consciousness is only too likely to twist this round and say "Aha! How wonderful! I was a High Priest in Egypt," whereas in actual fact you were nothing of the sort, but only a Temple servant of quite a low grade. It is a very human fallibility to build rosy retrospective romances which are very far from being the truth, and it is Truth which every sincere Occultist must seek with all his might.

If you cannot even trust your ordinary memory in this life, how much less can you depend on odd "flashes" which you take to be (perhaps correctly) of other lives? Neither seek nor shun such "flashes." Simply treat them as part and parcel of your conscious experience if and when they arrive, noting and studying them as they stand, but not letting them bother or interfere with your conscious living of this life in any way.

To use the teaching of reincarnation wisely from an Occult angle, apply it to this life by realising the mistakes you make, and the faults you have, resolving to do better and correct yourself in the future, both in this life and the next. That will be of practical and positive help to you. To waste valuable time in dreams of past events is of no value to anyone, unless they use such memories to avoid future errors. That would be an unlikely event, since human beings are not anxious to be conscious of their own faults, and only choose to remember the "nice bits" about themselves, often making these much nicer than they really were.

In dealing with reincarnation then, act sensibly and do not let the idea disturb your balance. If you have no memories of other lives at all that you know of, do not trouble yourself in the very least on that account. The Higher Consciousness towards which you are progressing will take care of all such things in due course. What matters to you is that you have this life to live, and the better you live it, the better your whole future will obviously be.

Now it is time to examine the next letter.

LETTER 9

Dear friend and Brother,

I could not reply before now, owing to having had a most difficult time. Nevertheless, out of chaos and muddle, I have produced fair running order.

Now what I want you to learn is that he who cannot control himself, is unable to control others. One can only help and control others when doing so for their own good and interest. That is no mean feat, and requires unlimited practice and experience.

Such was, and always will be, the real activity of the Brotherhood. We do not merely try to develop ourselves spiritually, and keep aloof from the rest of humanity. That is a fallacy. Emphatically I must impress upon you that *everyone* is your brother, even your enemies and the worst types of humans. So we must mix with all. By the very act of so mixing, one influences them by ones radiations, which affect them very powerfully indeed. Untold times I have experienced this, and it is a power for good.

To keep secluded and comparatively protected is easy, but to be with all in this world all the time while working inwardly and outwardly, is not easy, and does require superhuman effort. Why do you suppose God put us *here* in this world? To be active, to work, and to help the less learned and the less strong, the less evolved, and even the living half-dead. We have to rouse them, help them, by visible and invisible means. Mostly the latter, for that is the better way, for they do not notice it, and so become more self reliant.

All this is a great work, and a delight for every Brother, when he gets results for others without being noticed. We are satisfied to accumulate power for Good, and disperse strife and disharmony, transmuting discordant forces into beneficial currents and channels. Do you realise what this means? It requires hard work, endurance, patience, and an inward spirit of humility. Only experience ripens, strengthens, and brings realisation. Speculation and theory is mostly useless. Better to do little and get good results, than to go to extremes and exhaust oneself quickly in the achievement of practically nothing.

Watch, think over, and assimilate everything. In other words, digest your experiences mentally, and turn them into spiritual growth. That is training to become a superhuman being, and your develop or retardation is *your own doing*, and the God-in-You will help you. That is the skeleton key to the subject. Now I close, for it is 2 a.m.

Best wishes and Peace.

COMMENT

This letter raises a most interesting a most interesting point indeed, namely the Occult influence of radiation. It is a very highly important subject indeed, for it is the key to the workings of Occult forces and powers.

The study of radiations is a branch of physical science by itself, and a working understanding of the physical meaning of radiation will help greatly in appreciating the Occult side of the subject.

Speaking very broadly, radiation may be considered as the emission of energy from a source of power through some medium of space. Heat, light, and magnetism are all physical examples of radiant power. For our present purpose, we may think of radiations as forces which are *given out* from their point of origin through whatever appropriate medium may surround that point in Space.

Occult science asserts that every human being is a source of radiant energy, and is capable of receiving energies radiated from other sources. It is with radiations of this sort that we are directly concerned at the present moment. If you are unaccustomed to thinking of yourself as a radiator of energy all around you, then you had better start doing so now, and get a realisation of your own possibilities.

To start with, from a purely physical angle, you radiate heat in all directions from your physical body. That can be photographed on plates which are sensitive to heat rays, so you can find physical evidence of that if you wish to. The radiations of a more Occult nature are not recordable by any mechanical instrument yet invented, and until such is possible, we shall have to continue our investigations them by means of our own superphysical senses.

Thought, for example is a radiant power. Hence the faculty of telepathy. Vitality is radiant, hence the cures by "magnetic healing." In fact, there are all sorts of radiant forces working in and through you, all of which we believe to be traceable back to the One Source of Power behind the whole Universe Whom men call God.

How often do you read that how hackneyed expression "He (or She) was *radiant*, etc.," and pay no especial attention to the phrase because it is so familiar? Yet it is no mere figure of speech, but *literally true!* In such an instance, it simply means that the person was *especially* radiant, on account of some particular joy or pleasure. You are, of course, radiant all the time to some degree. The more energy you put forth, then the more radiant you are, and vice versa. When you are in bounding good health and spirits, you can literally *feel* the exhilarating sensation of all your physical and superphysical forces radiating out from you in glorious streams. When you are miserable, and in poor health, you can then actually feel the sort of "shrinking into yourself" that such a devitalised condition causes, owing to great loss of radiant energy. You can soon convince yourself of the reality of your own radiations if you think carefully about them!

The Occultist is especially interested in radiations, because he realises full well how much can be done with them, and what tremendous effects they can have if used correctly. Again, they can be used either for Good or Evil, so great care is necessary in dealing with them. Radiation is Power, and should be treated with the respect and caution it deserves. Never treat radiations of any kind, physical or Occult, lightly because they do not seem very perceptible to your senses. That is a fatal mistake. To show what even physical radiations can do, you have only to read any good text books on the subject, and if that does not convince you, here are two instances from my own experience.

The first is amusing. I met someone I knew, who to my surprise had on that occasion a severely sunburnt face which looked most painful, and had been dabbed all over with camomile lotion to soothe the burns. This being in the middle of winter, was rather unexpected, and I asked my acquaintance what on earth he had been up to. It turned out that he had been "sunbathing" with an ultra violet lamp, and never having used one before, had given himself ten minutes as a first exposure, just to see if it worked! It had! He was most peeved about the whole affair, and regarded the lamp as a deceitful contraption, because it had remained quite cold the whole time, and he felt no sensation of warmth from it as he would have done from the sun. In fact he never *felt* the rays at all, and so imagined that they were almost non existent. He knows better now!

The next incident is rather pathetic. It concerns a young woman I met on one occasion who appeared a most beautiful and attractive soul. I had great difficulty in concealing my feelings when I noticed her hands. They were a dreadful sight, withered and scarred as though they had once been dipped in some destroying acid. They horrified me in connection with such a charming owner. When she had left the room, I enquired about her from someone else, and learned that she was an assistant to a doctor who experimented a good deal in radiology, and that was how she had suffered such damage to her hands. I may mention that this incident occurred in a foreign country, so do not put any false construction upon it in regard the medical profession at home. That poor young woman did not feel the action of the rays either, until the effects they had on her showed only too well their destructive result on human tissue.

As an extra and final example. I learned of a case in which someone stole a phial of radio-active compound which he kept in a waistcoat pocket, until such time as he might find a use or a buyer for his ill-gotten gains. That cost him his life in a very painful way, for the rays acted directly on his spleen, I am told, and no medical treatment in the world could have saved him from the consequences. He too never thought of such a thing, because he could feel no actual effects when he first put the phial in his pocket.

Now, those and an enormous history of similar cases, are some of the effects of *physical* radiations. Because people *feel* nothing, they wrongly assume nothing is happening to them. It is a dreadful error to believe that things do not exist which are not appreciable to the ordinary senses, or to think that what you do not feel or experience is less real than materially felt sensations. No Occultist is guilty of such a stupid mistake. If you are in the least inclined to think that way, then correct yourself immediately. The proof is literally all around you in innumerable forms. Occupying the same space where you are now, apart from any other radiations, are those of all the radio stations which are transmitting their messages all over the world. Do you suppose they have no existence, because they are imperceptible to your normal senses? A sensitive wireless set will give you an answer to that!

So with Occult radiations. Do not suppose because you do not *feel* their action, that they are not working. They *are*, and they have a very positive effect upon yourself, whether you realise that fact or not. Your very life is dependant upon radiation, and without it you could have no existence at all. If you did not receive the radiant energy from Spiritual and superphysical Sources, you could have no consciousness or any faculty whatever. Our entire Universe itself is dependant on the radiant Power of the Supreme Intelligence which brought it into being. Radiation is fundamental principle of Existence, so you cannot afford to ignore it or treat it lightly.

Actually, you are living in a kind of "sea" of radiations, which are whirling and vibrating all round you in their respective ethers or space-mediums. They are of every description and type, from the lowest physical to the Highest Spiritual. You have your being within them, and respond to such as you may be receptive towards, in any part of yourself. They affect you in every possible way, and you, in your turn, send off more radiations out of yourself into the general stream which all go into its composition and complexity. At first thought, the whole picture presents a most confusing structure to an exploring mind, and requires a good deal of getting used to. One is tempted to ask "If they are all mixed up everywhere, how can they possibly make sense *anywhere?*" Luckily, we have the physical analogy of radio to improve our understanding of the question.

The reason why you are able to choose any one particular radio programme out of the electro-etheric tangle, is because each transmitter has a frequency of its own, which it is bound to observe by international agreement. When you tune your receiver to that especial frequency, it, and none other, is the one your radio set will respond to, providing the set itself is sufficiently selective.

So with Occult radiations. Like a wireless, you send and receive them according to the range within your sensitivity. If you are particularly susceptible to certain types and frequencies of thought rays, those are the ones with which you will be most active. The "tuning in" depends upon yourself, as does the "sending out."

It is an essential part of Occult training to learn the action and management of these superphysical radiations. Their uses are of the very highest value. Just as by means of your radio, you can listen to the great musicians and orators of this world, so also can you by the "Occult radio" listen to "Higher Intelligences" and "celestial music" by which your consciousness may be correspondingly enlarged. As against that, you may "tune in" to the most worthless rubbish, just as you can with your material radio. Discrimination and judgement is necessary both with physical and Occult radio.

Occultism teaches how to deal with the atmosphere of supernormal radiations in which we live. At first, one learns to be selective, and receive only good and pure influences, excluding all harmful or evil ones. In an advanced stage of Initiation, it becomes the duty of an Initiate to receive both good and evil radiations into himself, of which he will select the evil, neutralise it as such, and reissue its radiant energy again in a good form. This is a great responsibility and a tremendous work, calling for immense spiritual strength and effort. It is what the Bible meant by "returning good for evil." To a certain extent by no means without value, everyone does this when they subdue some wrong thought or tendency in themselves, and alter it into a good impulse instead.

Whatever you think or do, causes a radiation of some kind to "go out from you" and make "etheric waves" through Spade and Time, which are capable of affecting anyone else who may be sensitive to them. Conversely, you yourself are affected by other people's radiations, as well as those from sources on different planes. A radiant force tuned to a frequency of some evil nature, will surge around through its etheric medium influencing what, or whosoever, is responsive to it. So will a good one. Moreover, these radiations can be "stored" to a certain extent, even by means of material objects, so that anyone sufficiently sensitive can detect them. This is the principle of "psychometry," a practice in which the sensitive person is able to describe people and influences which have been associated with some physical thing such as a ring, letter, or almost any object.

Radiations are also mainly responsible for what has been called the "atmosphere" of any place. Thought, emotional, and vital forces have their effect on physical matter which is constantly exposed to their action. This accounts for many "haunted houses," where wicked or evil persons have lived, and impregnated the very building itself with the horrible emanations of their debased natures. Because of this peculiarity inherent in matter, the original idea of temples was to construct a place wherein only the holiest and highest thoughts and radiations would be concentrated, so that these would have an automatic effect upon those who come in need of them. To this day, certain churches and temples may be met with which have the most wonderful "atmosphere" of peace within them, owing to the accumulation of radiant energy given off from centuries of worshippers. For this same reason, Occult students are advised to keep a special room for prayer, meditation, and similar exercises. When this is impossible (which it usually the case these days), then the next best thing is to set aside a corner of ones own room, or do whatever may be possible under the circumstances to keep one place or thing specially dedicated to ones own use for Occult development.

The whole study of Occult radiations is so fascinating and complex, that one lifetime after another could be spent in research concerning them without exhausting their possibilities. It is no topic to be "put in a nutshell," yet so far as individuals are concerned, it is sufficient at first that they begin to realise their own connection with radiant energies of a superphysical nature, and follow up the subject by practical experience as they go along.

The practical meaning of these radiations to yourself, is generally along these lines. You are literally surrounded with radiations coming from every conceivable source, and having almost every sort of nature. The extent to which these influence you depends entirely upon the type of person you are, and whether any part of yourself is "in tune" with them or not. Radiations affect or influence whatever is able to respond to them, and that effect is to a degree depending on the strength of the radiation, its duration of influence, and the responsiveness with which it meets.

Suppose, for instance, a radiation from some evil source connects with you. You will certainly find that some part of you will respond to its influence, but you yourself should have the power to neutralise its effect in your being by the action of your will which is equivalent to "switching off." Just as you can switch off a bad radio programme which you do not want to hear, so you also can "cut yourself off" from evil radiations which you do not intend to respond with. All this comes under the heading of what the Church used to call "temptations of the devil." So they are really, surprising as that sounds. There are any amount of radiations coming from evil intelligences, which automatically incite corresponding evils from those who "listen" to them. That is a danger of being sensitive to the influence of these Occult rays. The danger is not so much from the rays themselves, as from your own foolishness in allowing them to influence your life and actions. It is always YOU who are your own greatest danger or safety!

It is the same with good influences and radiations. These too are all about you, and affect you as you are able and willing to respond to them. An essential part of Occult training consists of acquiring the faculty of "tuning in" to every possible good emanation, so that these may have a beneficial effect upon the recipient. With that faculty is also cultivated the art of emitting good radiations all around you, so that they have a helpful influence on others. This is how Occultists are able to benefit other people, by exposing them to the radiant energy of good and beneficial power transmitted from the being of the Occultist himself. Because he does this consciously and intentionally, the power is all the greater and the more effective.

You may have noticed certain people in whose presence you feel much better and happier. Others have a disturbing effect on you. Others again, leave you indifferent. All these conditions have to do with the peculiar radiations emitted by those persons, and the effect they have on you. Once you learn that, you can begin learning how to adjust yourself accordingly so as to get the best results. On your own part, you should concern yourself with putting out from, and taking into yourself, only the purest and highest type of radiation to which you can respond.

There is no need to worry about *how* to receive and transmit such Occult radiations, because you already have that faculty anyway, as all humans have. What concerns you is the conscious handling and manipulation of them. These you can learn by study and experience. Common sense will tell you that if you will receive good influences into yourself, then you must put yourself in a receptive state to these. If you will transmit them, then you must willingly direct by your conscious action, so that the emanations resulting from your positively good state of being be sent out of yourself. The action in any case is always automatic, but your own consciousness greatly increases the strength and power of the rays.

What everything amounts to in the end, is that you are a *living radio*, having the dual faculty of transmission and perception. *YOU* have the deciding responsibility as to how this "Occult radio" is to be used. You can use it for good or ill according to your nature and inclination. Most people do not user it in a conscious sense at all, merely allowing themselves to be influenced by whatever radiation affects them. That is where the Occultist differs from the majority, since he acts and directs his forces *consciously*, in the *knowledge* of what he is doing. He can and does help those others by his radiations of good and God-given forces.

The often used terms "good influence" and "bad influence," in connection with a person, are literally true, and no mere figure of speech. You can be either, depending on the sort of emanations you give out. It is the true Occult and Mystic aim, to act as a sort of "relay station" for the Divine Principle Within, re-diffusing Its rays towards other beings, so that they will benefit thereby, and existent currents of evil and disharmony may be neutralised and rendered harmless forever. From this Perfect Source, the Occultist seeks his main supply of energy, and he can only do so by attuning his entire being until he harmonises with the radiations which reach him from the Divine Transmitter.

Though you will not be able to feel these Occult radiations themselves, any more than you can feel physical rays, you will most certainly experience the effects which they will have upon you, and be able to note the effects which you can produce by their means. Study and practice will bring you the knowledge you need for the conscious development of your own Inner Radiance by the Light of which alone, you may one day be truly "Illuminated"!

Here is another letter. Let us see what else can be extracted from it.

LETTER 10

Dear Friend and Brother,

I shall have to write this by installments, for I am working at very high pressure indeed. However, in spite of that, you will hear from me from time to time.

If you could only regard your experiences from the point of view of an onlooker, *impersonally*, then you would be less concerned and much calmer emotionally. Oh yes, I know it is difficult, but I am pointing it out to you so that you may learn the art of presence of Mind, for that is necessary to a developing Occultist. Experienced Occultists keep comparatively cool and collected, even in the face of danger, continually controlling "self."

Naturally you will have failures at first. You are bound to. Never mind, keep on, and every time you will learn new points and profit by them. In trial or difficulties, always ask the Great Cosmic Mind to help you, and await a prompting or an inspiration *humbly*. Do not be discouraged or disappointed by a setback. Simply rely upon the Cosmic, God, or the Great Limitless Mind, by whatever name you like to call It. That is the general way and practice of a true Occultist and disciple of the White Brotherhood.

To know, is to have power. Ignorance is the only shackle which keeps souls in bond. To learn, is to know, and knowledge means *freedom*, until one reaches the Infinite. Meditate on this, and you will be surprised what thoughts and inspirations you will get. At first, your progress will be unconsciousness. Understand this well. Do not think that you are not progressing. It only appears so to you.

After all, you must have all kinds of experiences, so that you can reach the realisation of what they mean. Surely this must be obvious to you? A high class object takes a lot of producing, and so does a high class human unit. Both are well worth producing, and are all the more valuable because of the work connected with them.

Actually, I am quite pleased with your progression. You are becoming more tolerant and have a broader outlook on life. Don't bother yourself about other channels, just go on as you are doing, and the rest will work automatically.

Yes, dabblers in Occult matters are a danger and a nuisance to themselves and others. That is why actual Occult training has been so closely guarded, and will not be published in book form for the masses. Only the fit ones are selected and chosen, and many of those fall away as the grades get higher. They are so enthusiastic at the start, but this wears off as they go on. Believe me, I have seen and experienced this too. Many think of acquiring power for their own ends, but they soon find themselves in difficulties, and wonder why it does not work! Well, they are stopped, that is all. Some of them would stop at nothing if they were able to do what they wanted. Those are often prevented, in their own best interests, poor misguided people.

Psychic development is only the lowest stage, and psychic phenomena, though most interesting, diverts too many people from spiritual development, and that is a danger of Spiritualism. A lot of so called "Occultists" are often victims to this, and if you try to help or guide them, they think they know better, and will not heed what is said. It is better not to argue with them at all. Simply leave them to their pet theories. That is all. Often they are hindered by their own obstinacy, and they have to pay for it. That is Karma. Then they wonder "why?" They do not even realise that everything is their own doing, and blame everybody and everything except themselves.

Is it a wonder that such people often fall into a slough of despondency and depression, and are unable to shake it off? Instead of learning, and trying to understand the truth, they start criticising and dictating as though they were masters and experts already, instead of being students. Surely this is an insane and stupid method. Do you see with me this vitally important point? It explains the many cults, and dissensions, and the thousand and one "isms" and "schisms." One is attracted by Astrology, another by Magic, and they have hundreds of ideas and versions of what they believe to be the truth. What a pantomime and a kaleidoscope!

What one has to do, is to steadily and patiently work with humility towards Truth and Light. Quietly, without seeking personal glory, continuing ones work with firmness and faith. Now you see what is required of a real Brother and skilled worker in Occult science. Quite a different picture to what one reads! Such are truly higher than angels, for they have to work on three planes together, physical psychical, and spiritual.

Now think all this over, and I have given you enough to go on with for awhile.

> Best wishes and Peace Profound.

COMMENT

This word "impersonal" is a horrible snag in the English language, when applied to Occult matters. One reads so much nowadays in Occult literature about being "impersonal," "Selfless," "desirelessness" and the like, that the reader can scarcely be blamed in some cases, for coming to the conclusion that he seems to be a nasty piece of work from the cold Occult glance, and the best thing he could do would be to eliminate himself altogether. Writers keep insisting on the "evil of Self" to such a degree, that readers are apt is get very discouraged, and think "Well, if I'm really as bad as they make out, there doesn't seem to be much hope for me this side of extinction!"

Now why should this misunderstanding arise? It is mostly due to the comparatively recent influence of Eastern philosophy upon Western Occult writings, which come before the public. Before Buddhist and Vedantic translations began to have their effects upon Western writers, everything was much simpler. Mystics held to the idea of a Higher Self which was Good, and a Lower Self, which could lead towards Evil. In other words, mankind had a Good and a Bad side, and the work of the Mystic was to eliminate the Bad, and cultivate the Good. This beautifully simple teaching has been so twisted and distorted by our "Intellectual metaphysicians" that it is scarcely recognisable at all under the spate of camouflage thrown up around it.

The horrid word "Self" has become a most unwieldy spanner in the workings of modern Western Occult thought. Since nobody can explain what "Self" is, the word can be twisted to mean almost anything to suit the convenience of writers. Twist it one way, and it can be made to look good, twist it the other, and it looks positively dreadful. Quite true. We can be either good or bad, simply because we are human beings, and can incline ourselves in either direction.

From the Eastern point of view, "Self" is an *evil*, and the Mystic Union or "Nirvana," has been taken to mean the "extinction of Self." One of Gautama Buddha's essential Truths was "Where there is Self, there is no Truth, and where there is Truth, there is no Self." All very correct, providing that one does not attach the ordinary English understanding of that word "Self."

When we say "myself," "I," "me," and such personal words in English, we have come to mean the *whole* of ourselves, even the physical body included. Yet we will admit, perhaps in the next breath, that "Selfishness" is an evil, and "Unselfishness" is a good. This leads to a confusion of ideas which is anything but helpful, and it is essential to arrive at some clearer form of understanding, if we are to make any real Occult progress.

To try and appreciate the matter, we must first of all be in agreement with the idea that there is but One Great Self behind all our Creation, and that Self is what we call God. All Mystic schools of thought accept this. Next, we must realise that all the lesser Selves (amongst which we must include ourselves), which necessarily exist within that Supreme Self, depend upon It for their beings. In other words, God is the whole of *you*, and you are a minute fraction of Him, in the form of a human being as yet imperfect in nature. The fact that God is perfect as a *Whole*, does not make *you* perfect as a *part*, and a tiny part at that.

Now think of what most people call "you," or your personality. That is to say the "Mr Jones" or "Mrs Brown" part of you. If you imagine that *that* is all you are, then you are simply making a very foolish mistake. Your personality is merely the earth-expression through which you manifest on this physical plane. In a way, it is like a suit of clothes which you put on for the benefit of your appearance. Very necessary and essential, but not more important than the wearer who is your Real Self. Without that personality, you could not exist on this plane, and the better it is, then the better your expression of yourself can be.

There are two main things you can do with yourself. First, you can concentrate as building yourself up as a powerful individual apart from anybody else, subjecting all the forces and powers you can for your own personal use. You can make a sort of minor God of yourself in fact, and believe that you have reached a stage of Self Supremacy. Were you the one and only individual in existence, this would be justifiable, and in point of fact inevitable. You are however, one in many, and those many are of the One Who is God. Therefore this first choice is an *evil* one, because by taking it, you seek to separate yourself from the Divine Principle, and use Its Powers against Itself. That is the general idea behind Black Magic.

Your second course is just the opposite. In this, you seek the Supreme Self as your own mode of self-existence. You realise that the Self which is You, only exists as such because it is an individual creation, *separated off* as it were, from the Supreme Self which brought it into being. In fact, You are only *You* because you are *apart* from God as an individual existence, even though you exist *in* Him. If you find this difficult to understand at all, remember that in your own physical body there are millions of individual cells, each of which are a separate *unit* of the whole which is your body. Just as they can and do exist separately in your body, yet comprise that body itself by their totality, so can all the individual beings exist in God and yet be separate units by themselves.

Being yourself as something apart from God, naturally sets severe limitations upon your being. What you amount to *as You*, is nothing much *by itself.* You therefore seek continuously to *become more*, just as a seed seeks to become a tree or plant. That is to say, you try and *fulfil yourself,* and it is quite right that you should do so, providing that you work along the correct lines of development, which lead towards the Great and Supreme Self of All.

Either you can develop yourself as a unit *apart from God,* which is *wrong,* or you can develop yourself *into* God, which is correct. In the first case, you become yourself *as You,* and nobody else. In the second, you become *yourself in God* and everybody else too. This is the Mystic way, in which you become one *with* God, though you must not deceive yourself into thinking that you will ever become God Himself. You are You, and remain so in all your states. The supreme sacrifice of Self, does not mean that You go out of existence. It means that you no longer exist as a narrow, limited "You," tied to the confines of a small individual being, but become merged with the Supreme Self into the fullness of Its Eternal Existence. It is impossible to describe this, for we have neither the words nor the consciousness to do so, and can only attempt the best visualisation we can of this supreme state.

As a clumsy analogy, we might say that in order to be "You" as a grownup person, a child must stop being "You" as a seven year old. So whoever wants to be themselves in a perfected state, must therefore "sacrifice" themselves as they are in an imperfect one. That is what self-sacrifice implies, namely the "sacrificing" of the Self you are now, in order to become a better sort of Self in the future. In short, it means *progress!* To try and "hold on to" a limited state of Selfhood and glorify that into a kind of minor Deity, is both stupid and wicked. Adolf Hitler supplies the horrible example of this! That is real Selfishness in its worst form.

Selfishness is a quality which *isolates* a Self from other Selves (including of course the Supreme Self), and seeks self-being entirely through its own individuality, indifferent to any other Self than its own. What we call "unselfishness," is just the opposite, for it is the quality of *including* other Selves (and naturally the Supreme Self) within ones circle of being, so that ones Self becomes an indivisible principle of the Great Self which includes all being.

Everything depends upon what you do with yourself. Whatever you do to make that Self apart and away from God and the other Selves like you in which the Divine Principle exists, is wrong or even evil. That which you do in order to grow towards God and other human beings, is good and is the aim of true Occultism. The whole "evil of Self" consists in trying to establish a Self *apart* from all the others. That is "selfish." The "good of Self," consists in growing into the Supreme Self *with* the others.

Look at the question this way. The whole Universe is made according to a Great Plan by the Master Architect. We have the free will either to fit our Selves in with that Plan, and help towards its ultimate perfection, or we can hold ourselves apart from it as far as possible, and do our best to make things go our own way. No plan can ever be made perfect if all those engaged on the work are all working to different plans of their own individual making. All must work together on the *same* Plan, if it is to succeed.

To be Selfish, is to say "I am the most important being I know of. Let all other beings fit in with me and what I want personally." In other words, a selfish person tries to fit the whole world into himself. Like ten into one, it just cannot be done, and if the attempt is made, the greater power will divide the lesser into fragments. To be unselfish, is to say "I will fit myself into the Great Whole of which I am part, until I become one with It, and share Its nature inseparably." Surely this should be a matter of common sense, if nothing else, and yet mankind thinks so highly of personality, that the aim of millions is to have nothing better than the limited Selves they are. By analogical comparison, they would rather have the importance of a minnow in a glass of water, than evolve into a whale with the whole sea itself as a habitat.

Thus, when an Occultist talks about "impersonality" he means that it is necessary to see the personal and limited aspect of Self in its proper perspective to the Whole of which it is a part. He does not mean self-disparagement and a hypocritical kind of abnegation. True impersonality is simply to see oneself in relation with other Selves, and appreciate ones position in the Great Self. That is the *real* humility. It is a simple and frank appraisement of ones actual state of being within the Great Whole. In a way, it is seeing yourself through the eyes of God for what you really are.

Impersonality means treating the personality for what it is worth and no more, which is a garment for You to live in. To be impersonal means to live outside of the delusion that personal forms are the whole of yourself or anybody else. It means to take the larger point of view instead of the smaller one. To be "detached from things" means to remain free from attachment to purely personal forms of expression, which are continually changing and always impermanent. That is because if you get attached to any one form *as such*, you tend to hold back its progression into something better. It is like being so attached to a child *as a child*, that you never want it to change and grow up. That would be a personal attachment. Impersonality is that which urges progression and growth forward *because that is the right thing to do*.

True impersonality is *not* disassociating oneself from everyone else and not caring what happens to them. They deceive themselves that they are "impersonal," and say "Nothing can affect me. I have freed myself from all the others. What they do is no concern of mine. I am quite impersonal." On the contrary, such people are guilty of a peculiar form of spiritual Selfishness which is cold, hard, and of the most personal kind imaginable. They think that they are "free from others" because they do not *feel* anything to do with those others inside themselves. Quite so! The reason they feel nothing, is because they have deliberately cut themselves off from other souls and Selves, and wrapped themselves up in a sort of psychic and spiritual cocoon enclosing a little dream world of its own, from which they will find it more than difficult to break out into reality once more.

To be Selfless and impersonal, does not mean *indifference*. It means to the contrary, that one becomes so absorbed in other Selves, that one cares *intensely* about them and their true well being. Hurts to them become hurts to oneself. Their joys become ones own. Thus, one becomes a *greater* Self, with all the experiences and consciousness of those others assisting ones progress. It really is a case of many hands making light work! Suppose, for instance, that you *needed* some unpleasant experience to enlarge your consciousness. If you were living entirely in your Self, it would have to come to you directly, for there would be no other way. If you were able, through unselfishness and true impersonality to share the consciousness and experiences of others, then it could reach you through those others if they too, had such an experience.

Consider the matter from this analogy. Supposing a teacher has a classroom full of pupils, and he has to teach them a lesson, which is to say he must lead their consciousness into a certain required state. What if he had to take every one of those pupils separately through the full lesson? By the time he had got to the last one, the first would have forgotten what it was all about anyway, and you can figure for yourself what a dreary waste of time and progress it would be. No. The lesson must be taken *together*, and all must share the teacher's consciousness as far as they can, so that the lesson be learned in the best and most economical manner. The whole thing is *a coming together* into a common state of consciousness by the entire class. To help matters still further, those of the class who are brighter than the others can assist the slower ones at the same time. Thus, mutual co-operation attains the result aimed at.

That is the idea. We have to reach a common state of consciousness in relation to the Supreme Master, if we are to learn the Eternal Lesson of Life. We cannot do this by remaining an individual Self apart from all the rest. We must try and help each other for the sake of everybody, which automatically includes ourselves. The Occultist realises that the good of all is his own best good also, so he works accordingly.

Think of the Occult presentation of Evolution. Life works its way through all forms in turn. As each form is finished with, it is laid aside, and an improved one taken up. Now you are a human being. If you are ever to progress towards the Divine Kingdom, you must lay aside your human state of Selfhood in order to become something higher. To try and stay as you are would be spiritual death for you. You must progress, or else retrograde to a point of perishing. What is the sense of trying to hold yourself back by clinging to your human expression as though it were the best you could ever have? This is the danger of "attachment to Self," that makes one into spiritual children who will *not* grow up.

Fancy a person who so loved their toys as a child, and the state of childhood itself, that they remained in that state all their lives. Such do exist, and we treat them as harmless and charming lunatics to be carefully looked after. Yet we still persist in refusing to grow up spiritually, and cling to the toys and treasures that gave us pleasure such a long time ago! There are far better toys and treasures to take their place, but no, we will have the *old* ones, and refuse anything better because we are unable to appreciate them. It is similar to a boy of thirteen who refused the latest thing in electronic trains, because he preferred to play with the bricks and dolls of his nursery days. Mad of course. Well, at least no madder than those who cling to worn out Selves and forms fo the past, when finer, better, and improved ones are available.

It is important here to touch on the difference between forms and fundamentals. A fundamental is a Truth which does not change. A form, is a presentation of a fundamental, or a part of one, in whatever way and shape it happens to take. God is *The* Fundamental, for instance, but humans only recognise various *forms* of Him, for that is the best our limited consciousness will do. Allah, Adonai, Jehova, Brahma, the Absolute, etc., etc., are all *forms* by which various humans approach God. A form is a *relative* truth to its fundamental. Your Self is a *form* of You who are the fundamental, and therefore only *relative* to You according to its presentation. To make a mental picture, a piece of wet clay would be a fundamental, and the innumerable images which could be modelled from it, would be its forms. No matter what the form, the clay would remain essentially the same. That is why you are told not to attach yourself to any particular forms, but to live in fundamentals, and express yourself by means of the best forms you can find consecutively throughout your progress, developing an old form into a new one as you go along.

This does not mean to rush wildly from one form to another, jumping here, there, and everywhere without any discrimination. Nor does it mean to develop a contempt for forms or be inclined to despise them. While human beings exist in a world made up of forms, shapes, and outward manifestations, and considering that we ourselves have forms through which we must work, it should be realised that we must deal with them sensibly for what they are, the physical expressions of superphysical forces. They are here to be used and turned to our full advantage.

We must get the best value out of whatever forms and outward appearances present themselves, and when the usefulness of these is over for us, then we must find fresh and better ones. Yet we must not be so attached to them that we cannot bring ourselves to part with them when the time comes to do so. That is the true sense of "non attachment," which is to say not holding back our eternal progress for the sake of a *relatively* unimportant form.

While there is use and benefit in any form for you or other humans, then it has a value in this world. That is why the Occultist does not sneer or criticise formalities and expressions that others find helpful. You may be tempted to "lock down" on certain forms of custom, religion, etc., and consider that you are "beyond" them, or they are "beneath" you. Never do that, for in the first place it may not be true, and in the second place, other Selves find considerable help form those same forms, and it is the help of others with which the Occultist concerns himself. You would not take a fluffy doll away from a baby just because the toy looked ridiculous in your eyes, so why attempt to wrest from others that which pleases and benefits them? Furthermore, the baby's fluffy doll is not really ridiculous at all, since it has precisely the same value to the baby's consciousness as your latest particular "treasure" has to yourself! All things must be seen in proportion to each other, and this is what real impersonality is for.

A genuine Occultist is in this world to *help* and assist in his own progress through helping others who are parts of the Great

Self to which he is attaining. He cannot do this by remaining coldly aloof from other souls, and letting them "get on with it" by themselves. Never be deceived by a mask of indifference which some people pretend is impersonality. It is nothing of the kind, but sheer spiritual selfishness. Impersonality and unselfishness is a going out of the limits of ones personal self, and not a retreat within those limits so as to make them a fortified area against all others. That is how you can test yourself. If your Occult studies help you to be tolerant, broad-minded, kindly, and develop an honest love of other souls within you, then you are going the right way. If, on the other hand, your studies of Occultism lead you to feel "superior," and in any way contemptuous or intolerant of your fellow creatures, then you are going wrong somewhere, and had better make the necessary corrections. The effect you have on others, is the best indication by which to watch your progress.

Treat all writings dealing with "Selflessness" and "impersonality," etc., with caution until their meaning becomes clear. Otherwise they will cause more confusion than help. Remember that words are also forms of expression, and the fundamental meanings behind and within them may be differently interpreted by different minds.

The whole study of Self is exceptionally tricky and full of pitfalls. It should be treated with the greatest circumspection, for innumerable mistakes and stupidities are bound to arise from its pursuit, no matter how sincere the seeker. Provided a sense of balance and good humour is maintained, then there is far less danger of serious consequences occurring through faulty understanding. It is one of the troubles in modern Occult literature, that one is apt to go to some extreme or other in connection with the Self, and come to the conclusion that it is far greater or lesser than it actually is. The thing to remember always, is that you are neither a God, nor a worm, but a *human*, trying to make progress along the Path of Evolution which connects both states of extremity.

Here is the next letter.

LETTER 11

Dear Friends and Brother,

Though you have the potentialities ready, these have to be carefully developed through your own experiences. If I told you Occult truths, you would not *know* them, but would have to either believe or reject them.

Everyone has his or her own particular course of procedure to go through, as you will find out for yourself. All you require is that I should help you—to help yourself! The rest will all come naturally to you. Do not concern yourself with my personality. The main thing is that I have to help you forward as far as I can in your search for Truth and your study of real Occult work.

Remember, what you find today of great importance and interest, will be a commonplace for you tomorrow, and then you will be ready for new experiences. Do not think that because you are not aware of your objective progress, that you are not active subjectively. To the contrary, that is where you are most active, and that is why you get the answers to your problems by yourself (as you think).

I see by your surprise, that you do not understand the law of incarnation, and think three hundred years close together. Not at all my dear fellow. There is often a far quicker return to earth or physical conditions. The fact is in most cases a very rapid return. Still, that you will learn all in good time. The important thing is that you make the most of your experiences, and develop your faculties so as to build better understanding and conditions for this and the next phase of life. It is oneself who builds and forms ones next life (form of life). This is known in Eastern terms as "Karma," another thing which is very little understood, and not at all to be taken in the fatalistic sense.

Why should you think that you have lost touch with your higher faculties? It does not follow that when one progresses one should experience a lot of phenomena psychically. There is a time when that stops altogether for a long period, especially when you are advancing in spiritual development. You must not attach undue importance to lack of psychic experiences. One can work very hard on the spiritual plans, without being aware of it in this world at all.

You mention a ritual of Eliphas Levi's. Well that experience cost him the use of his right arm. That shows the dangers of Magic, even to the experienced operator.

Now I close with all best wishes, and Peace Profound.

COMMENT

The first thing to note, is that it is no contradiction to say that although we are all part of the same Plan, yet we each have an individual Path. That is quite true. So long as we are separate individuals, each *must* have his own path which cannot be absolutely identical with anyone else's, no matter what similarities may exist between one and another.

A number of craftsmen engaged upon any project, will all perform their individual work in their own different ways, and yet all that variety and difference of work will be for the same purpose and end, therefore those people will be working *together*. In a pilgrimage to some holy place or city, the pilgrims will come from every race and country in the world by every different direction, but all to the same place and for the same reason. Thus although divided by individuality, they are united by intention and common endeavour.

It is the work of the Occultist to recognise and work for, in his own way, the common objective towards which humanity and the created universe are heading. His is the task of assisting and co-operating with the fundamental Unity, which lies behind all the apparent diversity of being. To the Occultist, the Principle of Brotherhood is not only that of Humanity, it is Universal. He seeks the One Existence in which all other existences are contained. He performs his part in the One Plan wherein all the performers have their own particular share. That is the idea.

Humanity in general does not recognise its essential unity, and all the various sections of it believe that theirs and theirs alone, is the only way to attain the ideal state of being which all seek for. All religions presume that their particular notions of God are the best and truest ones. Each political party supposes that their policy is the solitary one which can save a country or the whole world from ruin. To the Occultist, these differences and disputes have their solution in the One Principle of Being which underlies all of them. He recognises fundamental Good, under whatever form it may take, or through whatever personality may be expressing it. One person might express himself best as a Buddhist, another as a Muslim, and a third as a Christian. All are different forms adopted by different people for the same fundamental reason, to reach inwards the Supreme Self through the Divine Principle within. That is the way the Occultist and Mystic looks at the matter. Each on his own best path towards the same destination.

This is one of the main reasons why it is an Occult principle to help people in their own way along their own paths. It is absolutely against Occult ethics to try and "convert" anyone to Occultism, which is no exclusive sect, but a Way wherein all may find a common expression who seek it of their own accord. Occultism seeks to serve the purpose of human perfection through whatsoever forms any human may choose for that purpose. It is no tenet of Occultism that all men should do the same thing in the same way, and become regimented automatons. This world and the Universe have complex structures, and must be kept going and perfected by as many ways and means as there are processes and workers.

No material project, such as an ocean liner or a huge building could be perfected by any one class of craftsmen. All types are absolutely necessary. So with this world, and the Universe of which it is a unit. It is an Occult task to bring all sections of humanity to recognise each others necessity to themselves, which at the present time they do not understand. Suppose, for instance, that all the electricians engaged on a building project refused to see the necessity of the plumbers, and spent their time in antagonistic efforts against that trade. Is it likely that the building would ever be completed or perfect? How then, can our human world alone ever be perfect while Christians refuse to see the necessity of Buddhists, both of those refuse to see the reason for Muslims, and all the various religions, political parties, and sections of humanity refuse to acknowledge the necessity of each other in their own spheres of activity? Occultism shows how we *need* each others differences in order to perfect the Plan in which we are as yet but imperfect performers.

At present, human beings dislike each other because of the differences between them. Occult teaching is to the effect that differences of nature should actually draw us closer together, once we recognise the fundamental unity behind all our variety of forms and expressions. This may seem paradoxical, but it is not really so at all. Just as your physical body is kept going by all the *different* organs and functions within it, so is the Universal Body kept going by all the different types of beings and lives which comprise its structure, all of which have their especial functions to fulfil.

Thus, the general Occult practice is to help others be of help to themselves, so that they in turn can be of help to others in the same way. This cycle of events is not quite so complicated as it sounds, for its aim is to develop all Selves through each, and each through all, so that the progress of the whole is the more effective.

In the matter of helping people, an especial danger of spiritual selfishness must be carefully noted here. It is important that others be helped for their own sakes, and not because of oneself. Otherwise a serious mistake can occur, in which you may imagine yourself as a good and noble helper, whereas there is really a rather ignoble motive behind your actions. To explain this, figure to yourself a philanthropist who was so keen on relieving poverty, that he secretly desired other people to be always poor and miserable, so that he could have the continued pleasure of helping them up a little, then waiting till they were poor again in order to come to him for help. Think of a doctor, who wanted people to be ill so that he could cure them. Consider a priest who was glad people were sinners so that he could have the delight of "saving" them. Such cases do exist. Note carefully how the element of "Self" comes in.

It is a good thing to have a strong will towards putting wrong things right, but it is a bad thing to encourage wrong so that you personally may exercise your faculty of doing good by contrast. That is like saying: "I want people to be worse than I am, so that I shall appear better than I really am. If I make others poorer than I, then I shall seem rich. If the others were more stupid than I, it would make me look really intelligent." In other words, seeking your own self glory at the expense of everybody else. This is far more common than you might suppose, and you could easily be a victim to it through a subconscious process of mind. In fact, that is usually how it works.

Many Occultists make that mistake, and go hopelessly wrong. They want Humanity to have "Messages from the Masters," and suchlike, but only through *them. They* must be the "World Teachers," but no one else must usurp their personal claim. Imagine as a parallel, a group of surgeons fighting each other around an operating table because each one wanted to be *the* one to save the patient's life, and desired none of the others to do so. How long would the patient live I wonder? Luckily surgeons are not such fools, and know perfectly well that what matters above all else is the patient's life, and that whoever is best qualified or able to do the operation had better get on with the job as soon as possible.

The genuine Occultist knows perfectly well that it does not matter *who* carries out real Occult work, so long as the work is done as it ought to be. It is the work which is of importance to the person, and not the person who is important to the work. All that matters is ability and fitness to do what must be done. A real Occultist is just as pleased to see work in which he is interested done by someone else, as though he had done it himself. Why should he not be, since the benefit comes to him as well? This is where real impersonality comes in again. There also comes in the danger of thinking "Oh well, if it doesn't matter who does it, then I can sit back and let the others work." Not so. The good Occultist seeks to do all he possibly can, without applying the limitations of selfishness to what he does. That is the way.

The next especial point of interest in the last letter, is that it sometimes appears to the persevering Occults that he is making little or no progress, whereas this is not really the case at all. Actually, this is not in the least uncommon, and need be no cause of concern whatsoever.

What usually happens is that one seems to be losing, or else feels a total loss of ones "psychic" sensitivity. "Visions," dreams, "astral experiences," and all the "exciting" side of Occult phenomena cease, or become most infrequent. All the colour appears to depart from the Occult side of ones life, and the tendency is towards becoming rather depressed about this, and think that one is "losing the gift." Yet it is quite normal really, and to be expected in the natural course of events. To the Mystic, it looks sometimes as though God Himself had deserted the soul in search of Him, no prayers seeming to be answered, and no notice taken of the seeker. Almost everyone on the Occult and Mystic Path has this experience in some form or other.

Now, there is a good reason for this "cut-off," which is for the Mystic's own protection. It usually means that possibly with the best intentions, he has been over-enthusiastically forcing his consciousness towards the Inner Planes, and diverting too great a proportion of his energies and attentions away from this material plane. In other words, he is overdoing the pace of his development, and entering planes of consciousness which his experience has not at that time qualified him to work upon. Such development is naturally very one sided, and when combined with neglect of the deep, fundamental faculties, it can and does overbalance the state of any human being.

What happens, is that the eager Mystic forces ahead with his exercises and practices, until the natural result comes about that he experiences flashes of consciousness on a higher plane. He is absolutely delighted with this, taking it as concrete proof of his own advancement, and works all the harder to expand his consciousness still more in that one particular direction. In his personal pleasure and interest, he overlooks the fact that he is neglecting his development both on this material plane of consciousness, and also on the fundamental plane of Spirit from whence the qualities are derived through which human beings may become perfect.

We are here on this plane for a purpose, and have work to do on this earth amongst our fellow humans. While we are here, the powers and influences which we receive from deep spiritual sources are meant to reach this plane through us. They will not do so effectively if we turn them aside by directing them to other planes of consciousness. They must be directed as it were *through* this plane back to their source, so that the circuit be completed. There is both work and Karma to be done on this plane which cannot be done anywhere else, and we cannot escape from it by trying to dodge consciously into another plane of existence, before our duties and responsibilities here have been carried out.

There are only three terms upon which anyone may enter any state of consciousness. One may be a denizen, a guest, or an intruder. The first has a permanent right, the second a temporary invitation, and the third neither right nor welcome at all. Furthermore, consciousness is earned *in* the higher plane *on* the lower one. Before human consciousness could be reached, it had to be earned on lower ones. On this material plane therefore, we have to earn the right and learn the method of attaining consciousness on the next higher planes of existence. Otherwise, we should not be here at all, neither would reincarnation be necessary.

In the best interest of the Mystic and Occultist, his *consciousness* is turned back from higher planes upon which he is not ready to be a denizen, is overstaying his welcome as a guest, and is not wanted as an intruder. He himself is not turned back, but only the conscious part of himself which has functions to perform elsewhere. His actual progress is in no way interrupted because his consciousness is turned in another direction. To understand this, we can illustrate it by an analogy.

The idea is that of walking in the direction of a blinding sun. The light is so fierce, that it deprives the traveller of his sight, and so he sees nothing at all of where he is going. He can however, turn his back on the sun, still going in the same direction, and he then sees all his surroundings clearly illuminated and distinct to his consciousness, though he sees them retrospectively as he progresses through them. His consciousness, as it were, unrolls behind him as he goes in front of it.

It is necessary sometimes that we should progress in that fashion, until we come to a fuller use of our faculties and consciousness. To work consciously on two planes at once, and be effective in both, is a task calling for a very high degree of Initiation. To maintain odd scraps of consciousness on either plane, is to be effective on neither. It is better that we make progress with our normal consciousness turned away from the direction in which we are going towards higher planes, than to have that consciousness so distracted that it will not function properly on any plane. The time will surely come for each of us, when we shall reach a stage of development when we are able to be conscious in more than one direction at once, and live both ways successfully.

The other side of this case is an unpleasant one. There are certainly ways of forcing an entry to other states of consciousness than the normal one. Drugs, and certain psychic practices will assuredly produce results in this direction. The result is degeneration and madness. Consciousness becomes so mixed and uncertain, that the unhappy person is unaware of what state they are living in at all, and confuse the events of the various planes with each other to such a hopeless extent, that they become insane everywhere. There are terrible examples of this in all our asylums.

Even with a pure intention, the Mystic may fall between two planes through overbalancing, as he eagerly reaches out towards the one furthest away from him. This is where the Masters can help him, by gently turning his attention back, and closing the gates which he has pried apart. It may sound odd, that his consciousness should be turned back so that he may go forward, but this is the case. It feels like a very bitter blow at the time to see the doors of better planes than this one apparently slammed in ones face, but if those doors have been prematurely opened, then such an action is really a blessing in disguise. If this should ever happen to you, as it has happened to myself and thousands of others, then take heart. Those doors did not close because you were *not* wanted there, but because you *were* wanted, just as soon as you could arrive there in the capacity of a rightful denizen, instead of a guest who came before his time.

Therefore, do not *force* any kind of conscious development. If psychic or unusual experiences come along, simply note them and bear them in mind for reference, but do not let them disturb or unbalance you. Let your consciousness unfold naturally from within you, instead of pushing it ahead too far so that it will recoil upon you. Do not intrude into other states of existence, any more than you would into a strange house. Wait until you obtain the necessary introductions. Those will come when you are ready.

With reference to what the writer of the letters says about short periods between incarnations, I can certainly support him in two definite instances to my personal knowledge. One was born shortly after the 1914–18 war, and cause his English mother considerable emotion by speaking odd phrases of German during periods of unconsciousness, whilst a very small child. He said also that he had been a soldier and had died fighting. There was no question of his being able to get this from anywhere outside his own consciousness under the conditions of his age and position. The next case is more recent, and is a distant American relative of mine who is still a baby at this time of writing. He can just talk, and has startled and puzzled his near relatives by telling them of the "people he was with before he came to them." In his baby way, he said that these people were "mean" to him, that there were lots of other children with him, and that half of them were *burnt!!!* The poor little chap seems to have been a victim of the early Nazi persecutions in Poland to judge from his account.

To clear up the mention of Eliphas Levi, to those unfamiliar with his writings, the incident referred to will be found in his *"Transcendental Magic: Its Doctrine and Ritual."** It concerns an occasion on which he evoked a phantom which he believed to be Apollonius of Tyana. When the spirit appeared, he became nervous and pointed the magic sword in his hand at it. The result of this was a kind of electric shock which made his arm useless for some time, and knocked him down within his magic circle. He came to his senses hours later, and decided against any such evocations in future. The use of his arm was never fully recovered during the rest of his life.

Now let us deal with another letter. Seeing that there are only a few more, and that much of what is in them has already appeared in them before in different words, I shall take the liberty of telescoping them together into two epistles. Here is the first one:

---

*Levi, Eliphas: *Transcendental Magic: Its Doctrine and Ritual*, George Redway, London 1896.

EPISTLE 1

Dear Friend and Brother,

Shutting ourselves off from the world is wrong. We have to live with the world, and take our share of it, or more, if we are capable of the burden (cross), and so earn our privileges, powers, knowledge, etc. The rough must come with the smooth. More often the rough, but what matters so long as it is effective, and the Great Purpose is served? True, this is far from easy, but I have never known that great things could be accomplished by ease. Everything has to be worked and paid for, for that is the Law. The wise Occultist learns how to shape his and other lives by doing everything in harmony with the Great Cosmic Mind, Its Hierarchies and the Masters. That is the way to reach up to the Divine state and its blessings.

Book-learning alone and striving after phenomena and power avails nothing, and only leads to confusion and perhaps destruction in the end.

You are beginning to realise the value and results of experience, and how vitally necessary it is that we should learn the lessons of life instead of grumbling at its incidents. Often, different experiences prove to be a great blessing, instead of a setback. The Law is infallible, whether we understand it or not. Remember, there is a time for everything, and lessons must be really understood. This means they must be *lived*.

You see, my dear fellow, you are in the enthusiastic neophyte stage as yet. You became very indecisive, and decided to trust only to yourself and your own inspiration. To a great extent, that is correct, but are you sure it is always infallible? No, for you have not yet enough experience. Your reasoning may be all right from your point of view, but it remains *your* point of view. You will find out that you will have to change that fairly often, with the result that you must tear your views down and build them up again.

You see, I came into contact with so many Occultists, and the different good in them. There may be sometimes some not quite correct things about them, and yet they are real Occultists, and produce good work. Everyone in his own sphere is made use of, and more often than not, do not realise this at all till long afterwards.

Remember, always keep your inner being ready for good and progressive service, whatever it may be, and you will get along much faster and better than if you were aware of it at your present stage. You cannot analyse the Divine Will, only trust in it implicitly.

You are not yet tolerant enough. Why be anti this and anti that? Never mind if you think others are wrong, try and see their viewpoints just the same. I have gained great experience and valuable information that way, which I could not have got otherwise.

Initiation on this plane only goes so far, and then the rest must be taken on higher ones. Before you get to those planes however, there are many initiations and experiences to be gone through here and now. Until one has qualified for higher service, one cannot and must not penetrate into these higher spheres. One goes through the whole gamut of human experiences by emotion and gradual understanding. (Head and Heart) That quality is gradually more and more balanced, and *spirally* rises. The Voice of Silence cannot fail.

Think all this over.

Yours fraternally

COMMENT

Yes, there is a Great Law behind the whole Universe, which we cannot really disobey, because the very attempts we make at disobedience invoke its corrective action upon ourselves. This is the Law of compensation, Karma, Nemesis, Kismet, or call it what you will.

This is not to be thought of in a fatalistic sense at all, any more than it is fatalism that a stone thrown into the ocean must reach the bottom. Karma is simply the law of cause and effect. If you put your hand in the fire, it is Karma that you should bleed. Nothing can happen anywhere without involving the principle of Karma, for Karma in some form, is the automatic effect following any happening on any plane of manifestation.

Ordinary physical Karma, operating through normal physical laws is easy to see, for it is evinced in every kind of material activity there is. Chemical actions for instance, are Karma of this sort. So are all mechanical and physical phenomena. The Occult significance of Karma however, is mainly concerned with the workings through higher planes. These are by no means easy to follow, even in a general way. All we can do is to consider them as best we can by the light of experience and reason in combination with whatever Inner Illumination we may have.

The study of Karma is closely tied up with that of Occult radiations. Whatever we manifest on any plane, causes these radiations to go out from us and have their effect upon whatever responds to them. That has been noted already. The Karmic result is that whatever has gone out of ourselves cannot be recalled by the same way it went, but must work round in a full circle until it returns to its point of origin. Electricity is an excellent example of this. A current cannot be sent so far along a wire and then recalled again, but must complete its circuit to the other side of the battery. Moreover, the current cannot flow at all unless there is a circuit already provided for it. So also with Karma.

Using this electrical analogy, we can see that whatever we do must come back to us sooner or later, for the simple reason that if it could not come back, we should be unable to do it in the first place. Karma is thus an absolute fundamental of being. "What a man sows, that also shall he reap" is a true interpretation of the Karmic principle. It also implies that he could not sow unless he had already reaped the seeds which were the results of previous sowings.

Whatsoever we do or think, sets actual forces in motion which eventually "catch up" with us again. The action of this is spiralic, simply because by the time our forces return to us, we are ahead of the Time position we held when they left us. That is why Karma engendered in one life, can affect us in another one. Forces of a superphysical nature work through a different time state to the one on this plane, and it may be even centuries of our time before they return here again. It forms a part of Occult training to shorten these time cycles so that the effects of Karma are apparently the more rapid from our point of view, and therefore our progress is faster.

It is this time element which confuses so many people. If the effects of Karma were always noted immediately after their causes in our state of time, no one would make the mistake of thinking that they could "get away with" evil and wrong activities. People imagine that nothing happens to themselves in connection with wrongdoing, because they see no adverse results affecting them forthwith. By the time those results happen, they have usually forgotten all about the original cause, and complain bitterly that they have done nothing to deserve such a fate. Nothing that they *remember* would be a more correct definition.

As human beings, our Karma is involved with each others to a frightening degree of complexity, yet nevertheless it all works out correctly as it goes along. If an analogy is wanted, a telephone conversation can be called to mind. Two people connect with each other hundreds of miles apart and spend a few moments in communicating intelligence to each other. That is simple enough as it stands. Yet the network of wires throughout the various telephone exchanges which must be used, is of amazing complexity and has the most intricate nature. If it is possible on the physical plane, for the two correct wires to be selected from millions and joined together so that two humans may talk to each other, it is also conceivable that analogous junctions may be made via the far more complex nature of the universe itself.

Karma works through forms and fundamentals. Its fundamentals are unchangeable by us, but its forms are naturally mutable. Let us consider this as an example. Supposing it was a Karmic fundamental that the death of Mr Smith should come through Mr Brown. It depends very largely on the characters of those two individuals how such an event comes to pass. We will suppose that Mr Brown has worked wonders with himself, and is far too good a man to commit murder. Smith meanwhile, is deserving of an untimely end. There are any number of ways in which he could meet this through Brown without the latter being involved in a guilty sense whatever. Brown might be driving the car which killed Smith accidentally. There are even commonplace ways he could be the death of Smith without knowing about it consciously.

Thus it is true enough in a sense to say that no one can escape their fate, but it is also true to say that it depends a great deal upon oneself in what form that fate comes. The same result may arrive by good, bad, or indifferent ways. It may be sudden, or spread over a long period of time. There are many factors which modify forms of fate. A lot too, depends upon what intervenes between the point of Karmic origin and its return contact at that same point. This is worth considering for a moment here, because it is the reason for the much discussed injunction of Christ to love ones enemies and return good for evil.

We will suppose that someone originates an evil force from themselves which, of course, passes on to others during the path of its Karmic cycle. If it moves them to evil as well, that means now evil will augment the old one, and more bad Karma will come into action with obvious results. By returning a current of good instead of the evil, a whole chain of bad Karmic events which might last for centuries, can be stopped at the point of issue. The original Karma will certainly revert back to the individual concerned in this case, and all the more effectively so because of the boomerang effect with which it was turned. In other words, by returning good for evil, you cause the evil to recoil back upon the sender so that it has a punitive effect on him for his own ultimate good. Christianity is a most practical form of Occultism, even though it takes an enormous effort to work successfully.

Karma is no "vengeance of God," but a Law of absolute justice which works with complete impartiality. There is no question of Divine wrath or punishment about it at all. We are not punished *for* our errors and sins, but *by* them. There is a world of difference between these two words. If we sin, then we must suffer by it, because that is the law of balance and adjustment which maintains this universe in being. What we have done, cannot be undone, but must be *worked out* until harmony is restored again.

It is wrong, however, to adopt an attitude of fatalism, and think "Well, if I must suffer, then there is nothing I can do about it." There is a lot that you can do about it. The form in which fate catches up with you, depends very much upon what you have been doing in the meantime. The better you have become, the more endurable will be the form in which fate reaches you. The worse you have made yourself, then the more unpleasant it will be. You cannot avoid the force of your fate, but you most certainly can divert that force into more bearable forms than it might have taken, had you not altered your ways of living. In that sense, one *can* "atone for ones sins."

Humanity as a whole, has very naturally a staggering load of adverse Karma to balance out. For a long time it has been concentrating its force with still greater effects through every war. If we cannot succeed in changing its form within the next few years, the result of future warfare are obvious to us already. A future war is not inevitable, because it is a *form* of Karma, and therefore can be averted in advance. In fact, if sufficiently good efforts were forthcoming, the forms of our Karma could be made successively less severe in accordance with the progress we made. What applies individually, can apply collectively as well, in this instance.

This is why it is so important to deal with evil forces effectively, and prevent their giving rise to further evils. Do you realise that every single evil which you overcome, means that much less evil for yourself and the whole of humanity to bear? Suppose an evil thought current affects you for instance, and you deal with the "temptation" firmly, and determine on a good course of action instead. You will then have made just that much less evil in the whole Universe, and brought so much actual good into being. Your Karma, and that of everyone else's, will be so much the lighter for it. Remember, you cannot annihilate the *force* behind an evil, for force is a fundamental which can be used for a good or evil form of expression. What happens, is that you change the nature of a force from evil into good by the action of your own will. The force goes on as before, only it does good instead of ill. If every human being would consciously co-operate in this sort of activity, what a wonderful place this world could be!

This transmutation of evil into good is true spiritual Alchemy, the Stone in which is Man himself. In the symbolical change of lead into gold, be it noted that although the *form* is altered, the fundamental which is "metal" remains the same. With us, although we can alter our nature and form from evil to good, the fundamental of "force" or energy, remains behind us.

Perhaps I have been overstressing the side of Karma as a follow-up of evil and wrong forces. It naturally works just the same with good forces too. Good and bad Karma, being towards opposite results, have the tendency of cancellation if connected together. Occultism shows how an individual can oppose his bad Karma with the good Karma to which he is entitled, and thus "square up his account." That is to say, instead of taking the good Karma in the form of pleasant earth-experiences, or the like, he can forego those forms in order to expend the force behind them in liquidating Karmic debts which he has already incurred. That brings his Karmic balance level in as short as possible a time, and for that reason, some Occultists prefer to use up their good Karma that way. Karma has often been likened to a bank account because of this. You can spend it as you like, but you cannot spend more than you have! Only earned incomes are accepted in the bank of Karma!

Think of Karma simply as a compensating force of the Universe, which corrects any inharmonies which may arise within it. The way and the forms by which those irregularities are put right, depends upon how they may be most efficiently applied. If we provide good channels for Karmic force to work through, then we have no cause to fear it at all. If we only make evil channels, then we have no complaint if Karma works that way. We cannot avert its Power, but we can provide it with painless paths to ourselves if we make the requisite efforts.

It is foolish to think of Karma as being confined to any especial forms of expression. That is to say, it must not be supposed that because our friend Smith has murdered his enemy Brown in one life, it must work out that Smith gets killed by Brown in the next incarnation. Things *might* work that way, but there is no *must* about it. In fact, it would be a bad thing if Karma were repaid on these literal terms, because that would mean no real progress had been made by the individuals concerned.

If Karma had to work entirely on these repercussive lines, then the Universe would be nothing better than a completely soulless mechanism. Everything would repeat itself over and over again in exactly the same way, and no improvements or progress could be possible. The main thing which saves this horrible picture from becoming a reality, is the factor of *free-will* acting through individually created souls.

It is true enough, that given similar circumstances, humans will tend to act in a way similar to previous occasions. This is natural enough, and understandable, but at the same time it is scarcely desirable from a progressive standpoint. If we re-acted the same way to similar things for life after life, how should we ever reach a state of perfection? The answer is to introduce our own wills into the active conduct of our lives, and prevent those lives from becoming mechanical cycles of repetition. Yet, seeing that habit and rhythm are such an essential part of our being, how are we to reconcile anything that repeats itself, with the elements of progress?

The answer lies in forms and fundamentals. Both rhythm and habit are fundamentals, but as such, they can be made to take any successive variety of forms. That is why a habit must not be thought of so doing the same thing every time, but as doing something a little better every time, and consequently changing its form through an improving scale of evolution. Such is the Occult idea, and the method by which progress comes in through the action of Will.

So then with Karma. Based on rhythmic fundamentals, it is our task to make continual progress, so that the cycles of rhythm become a *spiral* to us, instead of closed circles trapping us within their circuits. It rest with ourselves. Either we can spin round in Karmic circles of Time, or by the firm use of our wills, we can rise through them by progressive spiral paths, as it were, in an upwards direction, until we reach the Attainment which frees us from them altogether. This is represented in Occult Symbology as a serpent coiled around a staff or sword. The sword represents the Straight Path of Initiation, through the dangerous encirclement of the serpentine coils of Karmic action. Not that Karma itself is a danger, but it is dangerous to our own progress and perfection if we allow ourselves to be overcome by it.

The next point to note in the last letter, is that of seeing other people's viewpoints. Every Occultist knows the practical value of this to himself, and the widening effect it has on his own experience. This is the reason why we should overcome the hindering factor of personal prejudice, which only causes loss to ourselves.

Here is where true impersonality is of inestimable help. By its means, we can examine other peoples viewpoints without letting them affect us, and getting all the benefit of enlarged knowledge in the process. The Occultist scores heavily when he learns how to use this faculty. It is simply an ability to examine someone else's processes without putting any of ones own energy into them, or taking any out. In short, it is plain understanding, correctly used.

Prejudice is a great barrier to progress, because it is a self-imposed limitation to knowledge, and must be lifted if we are to pass along the Path of Intelligence. The basis of prejudice is mainly fear of some kind, arising through ignorance, from the purely personal part of onself. It is instinctive, rather than intelligent. There is always some personal connection where prejudice is concerned, and since this rarely comes to the surface of consciousness by itself, it must be probed for, and brought out for an inspection by the enquiring mind of the Occultist.

A condition of prejudice often arises after some normally unaccountable dislike has been experienced in connection with another person or condition of being. One feels "repelled" from whatever it may be, and the aftermath becomes a state of prejudice. Instead of allowing himself to fall into this state, the Occultist immediately wants to know *why* he should have the feeling of revulsion in the first place. There may be a good reason for it so far as he is concerned, and therefore he investigates the matter as deeply as he can. Perhaps there is some danger ahead of him, and he is receiving a subconscious warning of it. Whatever the cause, an Occultist must not let its effect on himself become prejudice, but instead he must turn it into knowledge, which, if necessary, can be translated into terms of positive action.

It is therefore essential to keep an open mind, examining everyone and everything with but one object, to get the truth for what it is worth in itself. That is the Occult aim. Truth is entirely unapproachable through prejudice or antagonism, hence these must not be permitted to overcloud the workings of intelligence and reason.

Now we come to the last letter (epistle).

EPISTLE 2

Dear Friend and Brother,

Several times I have tried to get you mentally, but you simply thought about me, and did not get the message at all. You seem to be too restless. Why? Try to be a little calmer, for you are hindering yourself by your disturbed condition of mind.

Do you know, you remind me of one of the enthusiastic disciples of Confucius, because you want to get ahead too quickly. Quick thought is suitable for your kind of wordly job, but not for Occultism. There, it is the reverse, steady and deep. Try that, and you will get rich experience from it.

What I have learned, is first to control myself—then others. Self-conquest is the basis of all Mystical training, and that is what we have to do. Gain balance in every state and circumstance. Emotion, Willpower, and Thought rightly handled is the sum-total. Those forces have to be controlled, or else they control us, and make us suffer, and can even destroy.

If a strong and mighty force sweeps past, whether it be misfortune, ill-health, or even minor handicaps, then bend beneath it, but *do not give way*. This is like the sheaf of grass that came upright again after the storm was over. That is going with Nature. I have always found it so. There is no use trying to force things. God knows how hard it is to be patient and humble inwardly without being weak and sentimental. To show a calm face and attitude, and not allow emotion to carry one away, leaving one exhausted and weak. The forces behind Nature are incredibly powerful, and most of the old Occult writers deified and personified them. Now we have all the trouble of clearing those blinds and veils away in order to approach the truth as it really is.

It is much better for you that you should stick to the Mystic Path, and keep away from all these letter and number twisters. Their intellect has gone top-heavy. They twist and they twist until they make wrong look right, and right look wrong. It makes me smile grimly. Never mind, we are living in interesting times, and things are slowly coming to a head, when all those vainglorious words will be swept away and forgotten. Nothing can stand against

Truth. There is worse to come yet. Many of us are trained and developed for tasks assigned to us, and must be ready when the time comes.

I send you a list of some Occult books, which I hope you will get the value from. After all, books and literature are only guides to working out the problems of Occultism, so that each problem becomes clear, and then it will be no longer Occult to you. Occultism is nothing else but all that is hidden and secret to you, and as you unravel the problems one by one, you become initiated into this and that. See the idea? It means the grasping of the process of evolution, and the development of ones understanding, so that one may co-operate with the forces of the Universe. The more we get to know about ourselves, and our relation with the Universe and Eternity, and *adapt* ourselves to it, then the more "Adept" we become. There it is in a nutshell so to speak, and the outline of it all.

Peace Profound.

Before commenting on this letter (epistle), here are some interesting comments which the writer made in connection with various Occult matters and writings, concerning which I had specially questioned him. They can scarcely be classified, and will have to be taken as they stand.

1. "There are Great Masters about, but not to be made public and give lessons for money. They are only for tried and tested students who will become neophytes. That always will and shall be."

2. "Eliphas Levi, as well as others, deliberately concealed certain things in order to keep the profane element away. Had he kept to the Mystic Path, he would have certainly advanced better. The Martinists were certainly affiliated to the Brotherhood. That I am told from Papus, who was our Head in Paris, 1911–1914. I worked personally under him right up to the time of his death. Levi's 'Transcendental Magic' is good up to a point, but pay no attention to Waite's commentaries."

3. "All we hear about in a lot of Occult books, are the different stages of astral intoxication. That is my objection to that type of publication. It is the wrong way, and produces a lot of victims through the often cause enthusiasms of ambitious persons. I have often come across many terrible cases of this. Nearly all the victims think they are adepts, saints, prophets, reformers, and even Gods. Invariably a lot of mysterious trash is published, and mental and astral indigestion is the result with the masses who swallow such rubbish, be it pseudo-religious, or pseudo-scientific. Impressionable minds are easily swamped by the powerful astral and emotional currents and whirlpools which are set up by this sort of thing, and may be set back for several births to come. It is all very well thinking that God will protect one, but what about the free-will He has given? There is no use jumping into danger and then shouting "save me!" That would be an unreasonable attitude, for it would expect God to be a kind of nurse to human caprice and wilfulness. Development must be natural, not forced and artificial. Quickened yes, but not *forced*."

4. "All the great Teachers produced Illumination in their search for God, but that of Jesus Christ is the highest and most sublime method, and the greatest inheritance of mankind."

5. "The number 32 is a very important one. I have always found the life of anyone rather remarkable in their characterstics about this age. It is important from the Solar aspect (esoteric of course)."

6. "What is Christianity? The same as it has always stood for. The state of Christhood. The *whole* state in *unity*, combined with Love in its Infinite sense. Love is the selfless, sacrificing, sublime state of being. It is the sublimated state in Alchemical symbology, the rare gold, the power *over* spirit, and the control of all vibrations. Most Occultists fail to understand what is meant by the Power of Love. It is the

most powerful force in the Universe, and of itself is above qualities. One can only grasp the meaning of it according to ones state of understanding. Yet, if it becomes passion, in any form, that is where the danger lies. It must be controlled well by Wisdom and Reason."

7. "The material world is the Shadow world, or the reflex of the spiritual world. Think of the Astral plane as a mirror. To get clear vision, a mirror must be perfect, and the light good. Otherwise there will be distortions and misunderstandings. This means that seership must be gradually and continually improved, otherwise it will produce only imperfect results."

COMMENT

Thought currents and radiations form an important section of Occult study and experience by themselves. As you will notice, my friend could reach me mentally at that stage, but could not attract my attention in return. This is very frequently the case.

Telepathy is largely a matter of attunement between two or more people, but everyone is sensitive to radiated thought power, whether they are aware of it or not. Notice, for instance, the "epidemics" of thought which effect nearly every periodically, and set masses of people all thinking along similar lines. We speak of "brain-waves," and of things being "in the air" without realising how near the literal truth we are. However faulty telepathy may be as an exact study, it has certainly shown that there is a Space medium through which thought radiations can be projected.

Most people believe that all their thoughts come from "inside their own brains." That is only a half truth. Their brains certainly intercept thought currents, and translate these into conscious terms such as words, etc, but original and constructive thought is a much more difficult matter. It is an easy and routine matter to use any thought which comes handily to mind, but to *systematically use* accessible thoughts so as to produce fresh thought material for yourself, is "creative thinking" in the Occult sense. The whole difference, is whether you simply prefer to act according to whatever thought "strikes" you, or to deliberately control your thought processes, so that you can build them into higher and higher forms of consciousness. The first method can be likened to drifting with the tide of thought, and the second to steering yourself through the currents towards the destination you seek.

Nevertheless, no one can ignore the tidal pressure of thought, as it forces itself upon us from all angles and origins. In the early stages of Occult development, one becomes increasingly sensitive to these currents, and it is essential to attain some degree of discrimination as to their nature. Otherwise, it is quite possible to mistake them for ones own thoughts, and be more or less seriously misled.

Suppose, for example, some thought or other comes along and begins to have an effect on ones mental and emotional nature. The first thing a developing Occultist does under such a circumstance, is to say to himself in effect "Stop. Let me examine this thought. Is it one of my own, or did it originate from somewhere outside me? If it is not my thought, then where and from whom did it come?" In other words, he asserts his control over thoughts, instead of letting them control him. He must learn this art for the sake of self-defence, if nothing else, otherwise he would be swamped out by all kinds of stray thoughts, and his mental balance and poise would be quite upset.

An Occultist deals with thought very much as a craftsman deals with the physical materials of his profession. Thoughts, to an Occultist, is as real and "solid," as wood to a carpenter, or iron to a blacksmith. It is the "raw material" out of which he makes his perfectly finished products. Using the peculiar "tools" of his own faculties, the Occultist takes hold of thought and fashions it by the application of his energies into the forms which he considers necessary to create. These forms have just as much objective reality on their plane, as physical matter has on this one, and it is part of the Occultist's job to become "adept" as a constructive artist in "thought-stuff."

By means of these "thought-forms," all sorts of effects can be produced on the mental plane, and, given the right channels, even on the physical plane too. Unluckily, they can be used for either good or evil ends, depending on the original intention, so the exact method of their production remains a "professional secret," since it comes under the Magical side of Occultism. You need not worry however, about being bombarded by evil thought forms, because neither they, nor the good ones, can affect you unless you allow them to do so of your own accord. You cannot be influenced either for good or ill against your own determination. Moreover, you must be in a condition of sensitivity towards the thought form itself. This is why it does not pay to be too "psychic" or sensitive, until you have first developed the sound, fundamental qualities within yourself, which enable you to deal with psychic currents and thought forms in a practical way. Sensitivity which is unsupported by sensibility, proves a greater curse than a blessing.

Many psychics and sensitives say that they are protected from harmful influences by their Spirit "guides." Very likely so, but the Occult aim is to develop oneself so as to provide ones own protection without continually having to rely upon others. Protection is only a temporary necessity, and to treat it as though it relieved one of the responsibility of growing beyond it, is to hold back ones own progress.

It is a mistake to try and develop psychic powers and consciousness on higher planes, before the necessary grounding has been put in. Actual consciousness is normally the *last* factor which attends the entry on any plane, and draw an analogy from it. The first thing which has to be done, is to grow a body, or vehicle, up to a point where it is capable of existence through its own functions. This process is not worked consciously by the incarnating soul at all, and the evolving body grows before birth in a state of quiescence and darkness. Although consciousness is awakened at physical birth, years of practice elapse before it has reached even a commonplace state of development. The whole process is one of step-by-step advancement until full physical capabilities are reached.

In order to function on higher planes than the physical, it is therefore necessary to have a body or vehicle, which can exist upon them in their own terms of expression. This is the mysterious "spiritual re-birth" mentioned by Christ. "Unless a man be born again, he cannot enter the Kingdom of Heaven" [*John 3:3*]. Quite true. How can anyone enter *any* "Kingdom" (or plane), unless first provided with a vehicle there in which to function consciously? Knowing this, the Occultist sets to work so as to "re-incarnate" on a higher plane, while he still has a physical body on this one.

If he can attain a state of Initiation during this earth-life, so that he has a simultaneous existence upon another plane of consciousness, and can hold that dual state in a condition of perfect balance, then he becomes what is called the "Twice-born." Physical death means nothing to him, except a change of condition, and he thinks no more about it than an ordinary human does of changing his residence. Life, to him, becomes eternal, and only the forms of it remain changeable.

Just as before physical birth, the body in which we shall live here is developed within a physical mother, so before death (or during our material lives), the body is being developed in which we shall live "over there." At our present "normal" state of development, we do not become conscious in that "after death" body, until we have actually parted with the physical one. The Occultist simply tries to speed up his own evolution, so that he is able to operate consciously through more states of being than one at a time.

To attempt such a thing without adequate training and primary development is sheer madness. Occult history is full of cases which illustrate the dreadful failures caused through a consciousness which has been developed without the foundation of character and common-sense. Self-conquest and control must be won on the physical plane before an entry is made to any other. That is the only practical way, and there is no sense in pretending otherwise. There are plenty of "twisters," as my friend called them, who claim that they have discovered "short-cuts" to Occult success. No such thing exists in reality, and short circuits or energy producing remarkable temporary effects, are not to be confused with genuine progress of a less spectacular variety.

The truth is, that real Occult progress is a matter of sheer hard work and sustained effort. Whatever help you may be given, no one can do this work for you, and more than they can do your breathing or digestion. No one can really Initiate you except yourself, because your own development *is* your initiation. All that you may hear about wonderful "Initiation ceremonies" may be founded on a certain element of truth, but no ceremony alone can bring about a state of Initiation. The use of the ceremony is but analogous to the artificial cracking of an eggshell so that the chicken my have an easier emergence. It is most certainly helpful but by no means absolutely indispensable. Nevertheless, just as it is of great value to have a doctor or midwife in attendance at physical birth, so can the help and support of our Elder Bretheren in Occult matters, be of comfort and assistance during Initiations into other states of consciousness. Yet, all they can do it to confirm what you have already done yourself, and unless you had made yourself ready for Initiation, they could do nothing but guide you towards it through your own efforts. It is always you who arrive at the point of Initiation. The others only make your arrival more pleasant and easy.

Now comes a very important point indeed, which my friend only touched on very lightly—the Power of Love. This has been stressed most heavily in practically all religions and systems of Mysticism. "God is Love" has been framed and placarded so often, that few people take any notice of the expression, and yet it contains the fundamental truth behind the whole Universe. The whole meaning depends entirely on how the word "Love" is interpreted. It must certainly not be limited to a physical attraction between the two human sexes, even though that is one limited form of its expression. How then are we to understand it?

In its full sense, we cannot yet understand what Love means. Whatever it is, in the Occult sense it is the creative and constructive Power which keeps the whole Universe in being and existence. It is this same power which keeps physical matter together in a state of coherency, each atom and electron in harmony with the other, and all the stars and planets in their ordered courses. It can be thought of as the principle of "drawing together" and balancing everything into a state of harmonious relationship as a whole. It really *is* God, and there is no better way we know of to describe it.

Occult teaching is to the effect that before this Universe was made, a state known as Chaos existed. It can only be thought of in terms of complete disorder, total absence of Law, non-existence of consciousness and entire negation of Life and being. What we call the Creation, was the infinite love of God acting in such a way as to bring the Universe into a state of being, order, harmony, Law, Life, and all that we associate with His Inexpressible Nature. God, and God only, holds the Universe in being. Without Him, it would not be a Universe at all. Instead of being a Cosmos, it would revert back to Chaos, and that would be the end of it, ourselves, and everything else that is now within it.

Thus we have two opposing forces. God, or Good, which is Love, holding everything together in the formation of a Universal Plan for the perfection of everything, and the Devil, or Evil, which is Hate, working against that Plan in order to destroy everything, so that all may be reduced to Chaos again. There is an Occult mystery here that no words can tell, nor human mind yet understand. All we can do is to approach it with our limited consciousness as best we may. We certainly know that our only hope of perfection and immortality lies with God and the fulfilment of His plan through His laws. Taking our own point of view as human beings, the difference between God and the Devil, means whether we will progress towards perfection or retrograde towards annihilation. There can be no compromising either way.

To say "If God is Good, then why does He allow Evil to happen?", is to ask a very silly question. H does not "allow" it at all. It is we, and beings like us who also have free-will, that "allow" evil to happen. It is no part of God's Plan to keep the Universe and ourselves together through a state of dictatorial compulsion, but by the Power of Love, which means that all beings shall come together because they are attracted to each other out of their own natures and wills. This is Love in the real sense. Perhaps a physical analogy can help to explain it.

The analogy is a chemical one. Consider the affinity between the elements of Oxygen and Hydrogen which makes them combine with each other as the vital compound of Water, without which we could not live. That is Love in the chemical sense. Now take the case of any explosive, the elements of which have a natural antipathy for each other, so that they least shock is sufficient to repel them from each other with destructive violence. That is Hate in a chemical way. As a point of interest, it may be noted that elements do not combine in nature to form explosive compounds. It took the ingenuity of Mankind to arrange them in that form for works of warfare and wickedness!

Human beings can come together in ways which are similar to these. Either we can be *forced* together against our wills towards each other, or we can *come* together because of mutual love and attraction. The first state is an explosive one, resulting in hatred, warfare, and disruption, and the second is an harmonious condition, resulting in balance, happiness, and peace. As yet, we have not learned how to live exclusively in this latter, and ideal state, and we exist in a curious alternation between the two extremes.

Love cannot be forced by external compulsion. Human beings can be temporarily forced together, but that state of artificiality cannot be maintained without disaster if their individual wills are hostile to each other. Either they must grow together of their own accord, or else break each other in pieces with their hatred. Love is not a power which acts from outside anyone and forces its way inwards, but it comes from the Divine Principle *within*, and grows outward towards all other beings. Growth and Love, are in fact, inseparable from each other. Love is expansive, and has the property of attracting itself through all forms of life and being. Hate is just the opposite, for it is contractive and repels itself with disintegrative energy. Love is the principle of Union, and Hate, that of Separation.

Above all, Love is an intelligent power. Its true course runs through Law, Reason, and Wisdom. In its Supreme form, it is directed by the consciousness of God. It should be correspondingly directed by human beings, or it turns into *passion*, which is Love being released into chaotic channels, and therefore dangerous and destructive. Just as Evil can be transmuted into Good, so, alas, can Good also be perverted into Evil. It is easier to do Evil than Good, for the simple reason, that doing Good calls for continual effort and concentration, whereas Evil consists of abandoning oneself to the anti-Cosmic forces and allowing these to run wildly into Chaos. Good and Love conserve and apply energy purposefully. Evil and Hate dissipate energy for the sake of destruction.

To the Occultist therefore, Love is the great Constructive Power emanating from the God-within, and it is his responsibility to bring this Power out of himself through the paths of his own progress. To him, it literally is the Power which "overcomes Evil with Good." There is no question of sentimentality or weakness about real Love at all. It does not *yield* to Evil, but absorbs and transmutes it by sheer strength and endurance. Yet the peculiar thing about this process is that Love does not use compulsion on the principle of free-will! It simply directs the force of an evil will into good channels, and if the personality behind the evil will is injured in the doing thereof, those injuries are but of a corrective nature and reconstructive in effect. The law of Karma applies in Love as with every other force.

True Divine Love is a strange Power to us as yet, and works in ways which are most difficult for us to appreciate in any other light than our own perception of it. Often, it seems harsh and uncompromising to our limited understanding, because we cannot see the reasons behind its activities which affect us closely. If we remember that it is always constructive in action, we may be able to follow its workings somewhat more clearly. We must bear in mind that Love does not destroy. It certainly breaks down old and outworn forms, but only so that they may be returned to their fundamentals and reissued in a better way. Whatever it takes to pieces or dismantles, it does so with the intention of recreating and bringing into an improved condition of life again. Thus, while we have our present imperfections and faults, death is a periodic necessity to us, and it is Divine Love which is behind the change of state which so many humans fear because they know not what it means to them.

Love is not to be confounded with emotion. Love may certainly be the *cause* of emotion, but emotion is only one of its effects. A sudden outrush of the Power of Love through any individual, has most frequently the effect of throwing them off balance fo the time being. Few can withstand such a pleasurably intoxicating effect. The Occultist however, realises that the Love which brought the Universe into a state of Cosmos, is essentially a *controlled* and regulated Power. He therefore sets himself to regulate and control its action through himself. This does not mean that he uses suppressive measure, or attempts to prevent its workings. On the contrary, he seeks to use it fully, providing always that he does so under the full control of his own reason and intelligence. God, the Supreme Lover, works in this fashion, and those that aspire towards Him, must model themselves upon His methods in accordance with His Laws.

It is a dreadful thing really, that the word "Love" has so suffered through use in the English language, that it becomes a popular synonym for purely sexual attraction. So many pseudo-Occult groups have twisted its meaning round for that purpose, in order to try and cover sheer lust and immorality. Such persons play with the most dangerous fire in existence, for Love is represented as this element in Occult Symbology, and the burns they receive do not heal for many lives. None can escape the results of vice, no matter what name they may use as a cloak for it.

True Occultism stands, as it always has done, for Love within the Laws of Reason, directed by an Intelligent Will. The human expression of this, is to be patterned upon the Divine, and not upon any false code concocted by human beings who have no Will in progress beyond their own Self-limitations. Real Love is obviously incapable of injustice, and no justice can be possible without genuine impersonality and impartiality. Love, in the pure form sought by the Mystic, must transcend personality and the separative quality of Self from Self.

This is hard enough to understand, and infinitely harder to accomplish, yet it is the only way towards the Mystic Union which is the state of perfection aimed at by all upon the Occult and Mystic Path. The most that any human being can do, is to use their power of Love in the very best way they know of, and continually seek to improve and enlarge its practice through higher forms of expression. None can do more than that, and so very few even attempt as much. Still, a slow progress is far better than hasty ruin! The old rhyme "Love me little, love me long" has an Occult application which will reveal a good deal to a reflective thinker!

So at last we come to the end of the letters. I need hardly say that there is a good deal more in them "reading between the lines," than I have been able to touch upon in these superficial comments. At a casual reading, they seem commonplace enough, and I confess to being deceived myself in the same way when I first received them. The truth in them is not to be met with by the eye alone, but by an Inner sense of recognition, without which, they will seem almost trivial. To this sense then, I leave you, so that you may extract the residuum for yourself!

EPILOGUE

I hope no one has been disappointed because I have not made the subject of Occultism sound a very "romantic" one. Real Occultism is not romantic at all in the ordinary sense of the word, but is a matter of constructive endeavour in the planes of Spirit, Mind, and Body. It is very far from being dull or monotonous, but it is certainly arduous and difficult, because it calls for "uphill climbing" all the way. For that reason, the Occult Path was often symbolized as a mountain by early writers on the subject. In the ascent of a mountain, one can either work from slope to slope by careful stages, or else scale the sheer face by almost superhuman effort and tremendous risk. For most of us, the circuitous route is the only practical one, unless we develop the strength to complete the journey by the more direct and hazardous way. It is certain that no Master or Teacher on the Right Hand Path ever encouraged his followers to take senseless risks and foolish chances, in which the element of success was almost negligible. The great maxim they all taught, was to the effect that each must work safely within their limits, so that they might continually expand the limits in which they might safely work.

So many people are attracted to Occultism, because they think that through its teachings they can find the means of satisfying their personal wants, and of developing supernatural powers which will "get them ahead of everybody else." They may have idealistic dreams of becoming a "Great Master," or they may simply seek the means of dominating other folk and having their own way in everything. What is more, if they are sufficiently determined and energetic, they can certainly carry out their selfish designs up to a certain point, and become an obnoxious curse to all who are unfortunate enough to be affect by them. Sooner or later, however, they all pay the same terrible price of their folly, and have to start their whole progress again, plus the Karmic debts involved.

Have we not seen the consequences in our ordinary lives, of what happens in the case of those who desire powers for personal ends, and solely for the purely personal delight in using them? From a ruthless dictator to a bullying officer, is but a difference of degrees of tyranny inspired by exactly the same motive — Egoism! When this exaltation of the Personal principle is turned into Occult channels, the results are equally unpleasant to others, and repercuss with more deadly effect upon the individual concerned.

As a rule, it is useless to warn anyone who is absolutely determined upon using Occult forces for their own ends. They are so blinded by their apparent initial successes, and the fact that they cannot see any unpleasant consequences to themselves as an immediate result of their foolishness, that little short of personal disaster will put a stop to their activities. Nevertheless, such warnings are given as a matter of duty and fairness. Whether they are heeded or disregarded, is entirely for the individual to decide.

Even these Selfish successes are by no means easy to achieve, for there is no short cut to Power on the Occult Path. Anyone who believes that there are secret methods by which Initiation can be achieved overnight, is due for a most disappointing disillusionment. That is no more possible than for a seed to produce fruit without going through the whole process of growth. All that can be done is aid and foster the natural processes of evolution, so as to get the best results in the shortest time by using the most efficient means. Occultism can provide those means, but it is the Occultist who must cultivate himself through their application.

The real basis of Occultism is growth and development through consciousness into the ultimate perfection which lies before every human, whether they are Occultists or not. The processes of esotericism are those of consciousness itself, extending through every plane on which humanity must manifest before perfection is attained. The main advantage of Occult methods, are that they make for economy, efficiency, and the maximum safe speed in human development. Their disadvantage is that they are very liable to abuse and misuse, are dangerous in careless or unscrupulous hands, and are capable of injuring others than the users. Like sharp tools, they should only be handled by competent craftsmen, or trainees under supervision. However, there are certainly a great many Occult methods and practices which are sufficiently public to be used by those who will avail themselves of the means towards higher knowledge. The clues to this knowledge have been often printed and published. It remains with the industry of the readers to arrive at the answers.

Finding these answers, is a most difficult matter. Often, the difficulty is deliberately created, so that the answer to an Occult problem is only to be found through a process of thought and practice which tends to make the thinker and doer a fit and proper recipient for the concealed truth he is approaching. A good example of this, is the system of Magic written by "Abraham the Jew to his son Lamech," and attributed to a certain Abramelin the Mage.* In it, Abraham promises all sorts of wonderful Occult Powers over evil spirits, but makes the strictest proviso that before practicing the Ritual, the magician must spend six months in a semi-secluded sort of life, during which time he must behave with an exemplary goodness of character. He is enjoined to works of charity, reading the scriptures, and to almost saintly behaviour. If anyone fulfilled those conditions as instructed, by the end of the six months, he would have made such a great improvement of being and character, that a deliberate invocation of the Powers of Evil to work his own personal will, would be unthinkable to him! Knowing human weakness however, the clever Abraham lured his son and others towards the Right Hand Path of Good, but a symbolic promise of great personal powers over evil, if the rules he imposed were followed. Quite true! Whoever lived half a year as Abraham directed, would most certainly attain a high degree of mastery over evil—in himself! It is very significant that Abraham laid down no fixed ritual for invoking the Satanic Powers, but instructs his son that such knowledge must come to him through his own Guardian Angel.

Occult writings are absolutely full of such "red herrings," some drawn across the Path for good reasons, and others for bad ones. Certain truths are presented in an analogical form, and others are given symbolically. Sometimes a truth is put into such blunt and unmistakable terms, that it seems too obvious to be true, and

---

**Sacred Magic of Abra-melin the Mage*, transl. S.L. MacGregor-Mathers, Thorsons Publishers Ltd., Wellingborough 1976; *The Book of Abramelin*, transl. G. Dehn, Ibis Press, Lake Worth 2006; Patai, R.: *The Jewish Alchemists: A History and Source Book*, Princeton University Press, Princeton 1994.

so it is overlooked as a "platitude," or an "old saw." May truths are buried deep in the beautiful fantasy of fairy tales and legends. Children often feel this instinctively, though of course they are unable to put their feelings into words and thoughts that grown up people can understand.

Again, Occult writers of all ages have embroidered their subject with professional skill, sometimes from a love of romancing and sometimes because of a pompous desire to impress their readers. Few writers can resist employing "tricks of the trade," in order to improve the sales value of their work. This would be legitimate and human enough, providing that deliberate falsification were not employed, as it occasionally is. All sorts of genuine mistakes, misquotations, and unintentional errors, arise in Occult writings as a matter of course, and must be sifted out by the searcher for Truth. There is no question that vital and essential truths are to be found in most Occult publications, but the process of finding them is no simple matter. Not only has one to read "between" the lines, but *behind* and *through* them as well.

After reading fascinating accounts of Occultism, one is often considerably surprised when meeting with the reality. This must always be allowed for, in order to maintain a state of mental balance about the subject. It is like the glowing accounts of the "mysterious East," which thrill those who have never lived there! As small instances of how exaggerations can occur, here are one or two of those I have been able to check personally, and are not without amusement.

The first point was a mention in a certain Occult book of some "squares of sevens" which the writer found indented on the top of the Great Pyramid. He attributed considerable Occult significance to these. It is true enough that the number seven has deep Mystical significance, but those inscribed on the Pyramid are for quite another purpose. They were cut by Arab guides for the purpose of playing an Egyptian game called "Mengala," which is not unlike our English "draughts," and can be played on any board with an odd number of squares. Often, while waiting for tourists whom they are escorting, they will pass away the time with this traditional game. Since I was taught the game myself on those same squares at the summit of the Pyramid, and had my information from the Arab custodian, I feel entitled to amend any false impressions about those particular Pyramid inscriptions.

Another modern Occult writer wrote up a visit paid to the monastery of the Dervishes near Cairo, in a most entrancing way. The impression given by the article, was that the place swarmed with Initiates, and the writer was only admitted by especial favour. Quite a sentimental little paragraph was devoted to the Brother who met the writer at the gate, and looked "With deep, soul-searching gaze," etc., etc. Very charmingly romantic, but far indeed from being a reality. Anyone is free to visit that monastery during visiting hours, providing a small fee is paid to he whose eyes search ones cash value at the gate! Half a piastre admitted me freely one afternoon. The specialty of the Dervishes who live there, is to induce a state of auto-hypnosis by whirling rapidly for prolonged periods. This certainly produces a class of interesting, though unspiritual phenomena, but the Dervishes can scarcely be classed as Initiates in the real sense and value of the word.

Then there is an instance of a well-known novelist who writes "Occult" novels of a somewhat lurid type. Some people who read them are under the impression that they have been written from a large fund of personal experience in Occult matters. Such a misconception in this case is due to no fault of the author, who quite frankly admits that the whole material is drawn from traditional sources, and put together in such a way as to produce an amusing and interesting type of pure fiction. Yet that novelist wrote me, that after the publication of a "thriller," invitations to ceremonies of Satan-worship and Black Magic, were sent to the writer! Despite professional interest, these were duly declined. At any rate, proof was afforded that Satanism is still practised in modern England, but in most cases it is a blind for what are commonly called "unsavoury practices."

On one occasion I happened to be discussing Symbology with a member of a small Occult group. During the conversation I traced a symbol or two on the back of an old envelope in order to stress some particular point or other. My acquaintance glanced at them in shocked surprise, and informed me that they were *very* secret indeed, and exclusive to his sect. Where, he asked me, had I access to such arcane information? It seemed a pity to disillusion the poor man, but I had to confess that I had come across them in a book borrowed from the Public Library! His consternation was completely funny!

Now all these instances are trivial and amusing enough, but in combination with thousands of parallels, they do show what misconceptions and errors arise in Occult matters. The very natural questions at this point are "Then what *is* one to think about Occultism? How is one to approach and deal with the subject, so as to get the truth? What is the best attitude to adopt?" All these are perfectly reasonable questions, and have a right to be answered as concisely and explicitly as possible.

The most rational attitude towards Occultism, is one of sincere and open minded interest. The extremes of scepticism and fanaticism are equally to be avoided, since both lead in opposite directions from truth. Occultism is no affair of set beliefs and fixed dogmas that must be unreservedly accepted, but it is a living enquiry into the hidden laws of the Universe. The limits of Occultism are those of Consciousness itself. It is not easy to give personal directions with regard to the study of Occult Mysticism, but the following generalisations may prove of help.

First, read and study Occult publications with an open mind, without being influenced by them in any special direction. Simply note what they have to say, and form what conclusions you consider justifiable. Next, formulate from what you have studied and thought, a code on which to base your future activities. Do not, however, fix your faith firmly in any especial *form* which is connected with Occultism. Just accept a form for what it is, a temporary convenience for the manifestation of thought, and use it as long as it is valuable to you. By this I mean that it is unwise to say "I believe in so-and-so, in this particular way, and nothing will ever alter my belief." Distinguish carefully between forms and fundamentals, and while founding your faith on fundamentals, be always prepared to alter the forms according to your progress.

For instance, you may take Karma as a fundamental. The moment you think about it, your mind begins to make form impressions about the subject of Karma, and you think "It must be thus and so." Those thought-forms will most certainly be of good service to you for perhaps quite a while. As you make progress though, you will reach a point where you have outgrown them. Very well then, lay them aside, and adopt the fresh ones that are the result of your studies and hard work. So continue. Remember that a fundamental is something that you *cannot* reject or cease to believe in. All that happens is that you improve your knowledge of it through perfecting the forms of your belief in it.

Whatever else you do, maintain a state of balance so far as you can throughout your whole being. Do not become so biased, that you become intolerant of anything or anyone outside your personal conceptions. Occultism is not a study which *ex*cludes all other approaches to Truth. To the contrary, it *in*cludes them all within its scope. It is a religion because it links God with Man through consciousness, and yet it is no exclusive *form* of religion. It is a science because it concerns itself with exact knowledge of the Laws and processes behind all manifestation, though it does not confine itself to any one particular plane of being. It is a philosophy, because the Principle of Wisdom is approached in and through all its forms. It is an aft, because it requires constructive skill and individual application in its practice. Occultism, in fact, is a Fundamental by itself, for it is the Fundamental of *evolving consciousness*, and there would seem no end to the forms through which that Fundamental can be expressed.

With regard to reading Occult publications, these cannot be treated as though they were a casual tale, told for a temporary entertainment. To merely *read* an Occult book is little use. It is also insufficient to study an Occult work as though it were a text book which could be learned by rule of thumb and applied through intellectual means. The reason for this is that genuine Occult books deal with processes of consciousness, which are much higher than the ordinary one reading the printed words. Our earth-plane languages are inadequate to express the peculiarities of other planes than our own. Therefore, the best that any author can do, is approximate his meaning in the nearest physical-plane terms to suit his purpose. This is why all the great Occult teachers taught, quite frankly, by means of parables, analogies, and symbols. To take an Occult work at "face-value," is to invite deception and misunderstanding.

The whole point of reading Occult writings at all, is to reach through them towards the plane of consciousness from which they originated. Having done this to the best of your ability, it remains to formulate your own conscious impressions, and then put them into use so that they are of service to you on whatever plane you mean to apply them. Everyone has methods of their own, which are best suited to themselves for this purpose, but for at least a trial procedure, the following has a lot to recommend it.

First, read through the work very quickly, getting general ideas about it, and then leave it alone for a while, so that the material "soaks into" your subconscious mind. Later on, go through the book at normal speed, bringing everything into as clear a focus as possible, and formulating whatever impressions occur to you. When you are ready for the third perusal, do this with great thoroughness and with reflective thought. Use meditation this time, and make your thoughts bear the fruit of their thinking. Note down, if you like, whatever new thoughts have come to you because of your mental work. If you can find a way of linking these with your own life, try them out with the intention of producing a good result which will be helpful to all concerned.

Do not forget that your general development is watched by entities on Higher Planes. Call them Masters or Spirit Guides, or whatever name you please, those beings definitely exist, and are able to keep in touch with you mostly through the subjective part of yourself. It is very unusual for them to make conscious contact with anyone on the initial stages of the Occult Path. This is because they realise that if you grow into a sense of dependency on them, you would tend to slack off your own efforts. Their hope is that some day you will be a *worker*, as they are themselves, and take your place with them in the Great Work upon which they are most actively engaged. Never believe that they will do things for you, which you are capable of doing for yourself. It would not be fair to you if they did. They will, however, give you all the help they possibly can, so that you are enable to make your own way along the Path. You need not waste time in asking them mentally to help you develop any special "Occult-Powers," which you only want for the sake of having them. The Masters' first concern is that you be made worthy of any power, before you are entrusted with it. This worthiness has to be the result of your own careful work.

Therefore, it is undesirable to encourage in yourself any especial powers or "psychic gifts." Aim first at development of character and the Inner realisation of the Divine Spirit in all things. You will not be the loser, for the gifts and powers will most assuredly come to you in the correct order and at the right time, if you follow the line of central development, and in fact, you will not be able to avoid them, because they are part and parcel of a perfecting human nature. To try and develop supernormal faculties before you are prepared for them, is just asking for trouble. The maxim here is that before you acquire a power, you should first of all develop the ability to use it correctly and wisely. Otherwise the result is only too likely to be damage and disaster.

It is a pity that so many are attracted to Occultism because they only think of it in terms of external "sense effects." They seek for "thrilling experiences on the Astral Plane," and an extra life, as it were, in which to gratify their sense desires. Such people do not seek either an improvement or a progression of their sense faculties, but only an *extension* of them. Their aim is not Truth, but personal pleasure and amusement. If they do not find what they want in Occultism, which is mostly the case, then they discard it in disgust. Should they, on the other hand, hit on some method which gives them entry to the plane of being they seek, then there is no holding them back until they meet with an unpleasant experience which they richly deserve. Then they usually condemn Occultism with all their might, and cry out that it is dangerous and unsafe. Their cries are just as ridiculous as might be those of someone who demanded the total abolition of razors, because he had cut himself whilst shaving.

Occultism is either safe or dangerous depending entirely upon the user, and the use to which it is put. There is no more reason to be afraid of it, than there is of swimming for instance. Everyone knows that there is a danger of drowning whilst swimming, but no reasonable person is thereby deterred from doing so after taking all due precautions for their own safety. There is scarcely a single human activity that has not its own particular danger, from which reason and commonsense constantly deliver us. This is true of Occultism also, though its dangers are in the reverse order of those on the physical plane. Here, bodily injuries come first, and may have subsequent repercussions on the planes of mind and spirit. In Occultism, the mind and soul are first affected, and injuries sustained in those states of being may later on have a bad effect on physical health and conditions.

There is not the slightest need however, to start fearing and worrying about Occult dangers, providing a sane and balanced being and outlook can be maintained. Both fear and worry are to be avoided in any case, and should you "feel yourself slipping," the thing to do is to check your point of error sensibly, and put matters right in the most reasonable way you can. Have no foolish sense of false shame over any mistake you make, but acknowledge it honestly to yourself, and learn from it what *not* to do next time. Even mistakes can be turned to profitable advantage in this way, and there is no sense in losing the opportunities of progress which they present.

It must not be supposed for one moment, that the only sources of Occult information are books and treatises. Those are to be thought of as records rather than sources of Occultism. The actual founts of Occult knowledge are to be met with literally everywhere, and in every type of being. *Everything* is an "Occult Teacher" in its own way, because everything has its hidden or Occult side, from which you can extract valuable information and experience. Nothing is so mean or insignificant, that you cannot learn some kind of an Occult lesson from it. In one Eastern School pupils are given all sorts of very commonplace objects to meditate on, such as lumps of clay, bunches of leaves, etc., and told that until they can get all the Occult information which that particular object has to offer, the next lesson will not be given them. Fundamentally this is a sound enough practice, and an adapted form of it can be valuable in Western methods.

This problem of fitting Occultism in with our modern Western mode of life, is a very big one indeed. The only sensible way of approaching it, lies in the realisation that Occultism is no "spare-time hobby" that can be indulged in at odd moments, but is a way of bringing a progressive consciousness to bear upon ones actual living. Occultism is not something for "free evenings" or odd moments, but for the whole of life throughout all its planes and expressions. Occultism is something to be applied everywhere and at all times, in whatever form may be suitable for the occasion. Learn therefore, to approach everything in an Occult way, and deal with things by Occult methods. Only if you are able to do this, are you eligible to call yourself an Occultist. In the East it is the custom for those who devote their lives to Occultism, to live secluded lives largely spent in meditative and concentrative exercises. We of the West cannot do that, and so we have to express our form of Occultism through the active, difficult lives we have to live. This is the harder of the two courses, and calls for the greatest strength of character and powers of endurance.

To live an Occult life in our present times, and under the circumstances of Occidental civilisation, means that a very high standard of personal organisation must be reached. The thousands of details which make up an average persons daily life, have all to be synchronised with the Occult plan to which that person means to work. All the demands of such differing natures that are made upon the normal consciousness, have to be translated into terms which are appreciable to the Occult senses. Everything has to b e acted on, and reacted to, so that the net result is a beneficial one throughout the whole action. In effect, every different point of your consciousness has to be brought to a single focus, which is the fundamental of your own development towards your Attainment of the Mystic Union with the Divine Principle.

To get this focus with accuracy, you must centralise your consciousness around that Divine Principle within you, so that all forms of consciousness with which you have to deal are aligned with It through yourself. The symbol of this would be a wheel with yourself as the hub, the limits of your consciousness as the circumference, and the different forms of consciousness the degrees through which the wheel turns. Thus instead of rushing in a haphazard fashion from one to the other, you can face whichever one you please by turning on your own spiritual axis. That is a rough idea of spiritual centralisation.

This is what the Christian Mystics have called "bringing everything to God." It is based on absolutely sound Occult Laws. It means that with the Divine Principle Within You acting as your centre, and the Divine Principle Itself acting as your circumference, you are infallibly established upon the Eternal Fundamentals of Balance, Harmony, and Creative Progress. Since this process is the crux of the entire Mystical Path, it is entirely necessary that it be grasped in as clear as possible a manner.

Perhaps this conception can best be approached by contrasting it with the ordinary state of conscious affairs in which the average human lives. This entails a wandering of the consciousness in all directions, during which the Self accompanies its consciousness as on those rambling journeys. People say "*I*" am happy, "*I*" am miserable, "*I*" am sick, and they go through one form of conscious expression after another, with the element of "*I*" involved as deeply as they can entangle it with their consciousness. They follow their consciousness around, as it were, from one point to another, for all the world in the manner of the traditional donkey with the carrot in front of his nose. Their maxim seems to be "Where my consciousness goes, there go I also." The Mystic reverses this, and says "Where I go there shall my consciousness follow me."

Instead of rushing wildly about through all states of consciousness, and never getting much farther than any of them, the Mystic takes up a firm stand as it were in the middle of everything, and says in effect "I am sick and tired of chasing after shadows and making a fool of myself. From now on I stand fast in relation to them, and will deal with them all from this central point of my own reality." Since he arranges himself around the Divine Spark within him, he becomes not *ego*-centric by *Deo*-centric, which is the antithesis of the Selfish state.

The idea is to live permanently in one state of being which is constant in relation to all that is inconstant and impermanent. It means to become in oneself a living fundamental which is fixed, amongst all the fluidic forms of being which are mutable and changeable. Note very carefully that such fixition [fixedness—*JS*] is *relative* to all external conditions of consciousness. In another sense of spiritual direction, the Mystic is not fixed at all, but progressing as rapidly as may be towards the height of his Attainment.

The whole idea is exceptionally difficult to put into words, because it seems at a casual glance to be a maze of contradictions, but such is not really the case, because of the relative factor involved. Maybe we can make a conception of it through that friendly standby, the analogy.

In this case, think of a huge department store of many different floors. Let each floor represent a different stage of consciousness, and all the goods, etc., the things peculiar to each stage. The customer is the Mystic, and the Attainment in the roof of the building. He can get there by wandering through all the departments looking at everything in turn, getting lost in different corridors and corners, and working his way up the stairs at intervals. In doing this, he moves about freely, covers miles of distance, and takes ages of time. If he has any sense, instead of going to all this trouble, he will take the lift. To do this, he goes into the lift compartment, and while he *stands still* in relation to the space dimensions of length and breadth, he moves rapidly along the height-axis, which is the one directly connecting him with his goal. This is not a faultless analogy, but if it will give a general notion, then it will have served its purpose.

Put into practical terms, all this means that a Mystic is required to live continually in a state of equilibrium and poise, balancing everything in and around himself through the centre point which is the Divine Inner Principle. Thus, although he is fixed in regard to the constancy of his balance, he is mobile in respect to the direction of his own progress. In a way, this state has a physical counterpart in the gyroscope or spinning-top. The earth itself is a good example of the principle involved.

To maintain any degree of this balance is an extremely difficult matter, and can only be achieved with constant practice. As a conscious beginning however, the following exercise will prove infinitely helpful.

The first step must be taken in meditation. Calm the mind and tranquilise the senses and emotions. Be aware, as strongly as you can, of the Divine Principle within you. Arrange yourself around That as best you can, until you feel that the distribution is fairly equal in all directions. Then be aware of the Divine Principle in everything immediately surrounding you which is outside of yourself. Since God is omnipresent, you should not have much difficulty in realising His presence behind everything in the room besides yourself. Figure to yourself that a relation definitely exists between the Divine Principle in you, and That which is in all those other forms of creation. Realise this relationship as having a path of connection *through yourself*. Hold this state of consciousness until you get the definite "feel" of it. There are no words which can accurately describe it, any more than there are words to explain the colour "red" to a man blind from birth. Once you experience the right feeling, you will know it, and that is all that can be said in explanation.

Do this on a number of occasions, until you know what it feels like as a state of being. That may take quite a long time, but until you are reasonably sure of yourself, there is no use trying anything else. This first step is easy however in comparison to the next, which is maintaining that state of poise and balance whilst engaged in ordinary physical plane activities. To do this, you have to keep that state of balance and equilibrium as a state of life which you experience *whilst you are not thinking about it objectively.* Your objective mind must be turned in the direction of whatever activity you may be engaged with, and at the same time you must not deviate from your condition of Inner poise. This part is exceptionally difficult, because you are accustomed to swaying around in whatever direction your consciousness is turned. The only thing to do is to keep practising it until you "get the knack." Try at first in very small ways, and work up from these. Whilst you are walking along, or doing some routine job are good opportunities.

This does not mean that you should be abstracted, or "wooly minded" whilst you are practising. On the contrary, the consciousness must be turned with concentration upon the activity in progress. Consciousness, and forms of emotion may vary to any extent, and yet that state of spiritual equilibrium must be unaltered by all those changes around it. You cannot keep this state by only thinking about it objectively, because once you stop thinking of it, you go off balance again. Thought may be a stage of its inception, but it has to be consolidated into your actual condition of being, before it becomes a reality to you.

Therefore, once you have got the idea of it, try holding the condition without the idea. At first, you will find that you have to keep "pushing yourself back into place" with continual efforts of conscious steadying. The only thing to do is to keep trying and working until you notice sufficient difference in yourself to encourage more progress.

Remember that this condition of equilibrium has to stand steady throughout all external circumstances, so try it in connection with every occurrence of daily life. Both Christian and Moslem Mystics have a practice in common which is related to this. They remind themselves of God all through the day in relation to whatsoever they may do. The Christian says "I bring this piece of work (for whatever it is) to God." The Moslem says "In the name of Allah! I do so and so." This is certainly not without its effect, but what really counts, is the continual state of Inner Balance *through* which outer affairs are acted and re-acted to, yet without disturbing its equilibrium.

In order to make this whole idea still clearer, look at the question of Inner equilibrium as a state of spiritual health and well-being. Now compare this with its physical equivalent. Consider the activities you can engage in physically, without altering your condition of good health or even thinking about it objectively. So then with the spiritual condition. In both cases you can lose your balance also, and disorder is the consequence which surely follows. Spiritual equilibrium is a state of constancy in your own relation to God, whilst at the same time, all the changes and variations of life and forms of expression which surround you, have no power to upset that poise.

It must not be supposed that this spiritual balance is an unenergetic or static condition. It is only maintained by the continual application of power. Do not think of it as being like the balance of a pair of scales, which is held by the external action of gravity. If a symbol is needed to visualise it, the best one is that of the previously mentioned gyroscope, the balance of which is kept in place by the power of its own momentum. A short while spent in watching a gyroscope, or studying its motion, will explain what is meant far better than pages of analogical descriptions. As a summing up, it may be said that the Mystic takes the Eternal and Divine Principle within him as a fixed pivot, and revolves himself around that point, gathering increased equilibrium and stability as his momentum grows in strength.

The whole reason for this centralisation and balance, is because it is the principle on which ordered creation works. Instances of it are everywhere. The solar system itself is one. The balance of electrons around their nucleus is another. The seed, or life-point, around and through which living matter grows is an excellent example. The entire Universe is kept in being through organisation of all its parts around the Central Principle of the Divine Power. The Mystic, realising that he is a minute replica of the Universe in himself, therefore organises his existence according to the Universal Laws.

The attainment of this state of central balance, is the primary essential for Occult progress, and whoever will seriously take up the Occult Path, must be prepared to spend whatever time and efforts which may be necessary to achieve it. Without it no measure of real occult success can be hoped for, for it is the secret of spiritual dynamism, and produces the power for the performance of Occult works.

I am well aware of the sketchy nature of my explanations and analogies, but there is no help for this, because the idea will not fit properly into any human language I know. To understand the difficulty, try explaining to someone *exactly* how you feel when in a condition of excellent health and exuberant spirits. No matter what you say, the words you use will only have a figurative reference in the condition of well-being you feel in yourself. If the other person understands you, they only do so because they too have experienced that condition for themselves, and therefore understand it in you. It is the same with Occult conditions of being. To experience them is one thing, but to try and reproduce that experience in terms of written words, is an impossibility at the present time. All that can be done, is choose words which are likely to lead the reader to a point where he can make the rest of the way for himself. If I have been able to do that, then my part of the work has been accomplished.

Which brings us to the conclusion of what I have to say. Please remember that this is no attempt to tell you "all about Occultism," because that would obviously be a ridiculous impossibility. I have simply tried to show, to the best of my limited ability, that Occultism is a way of life which is practicable and justifiable. The true Occultist is a fundamentalist who seeks essential Truth as a foundation upon which he builds the forms which express those Truths to his understanding. With his whole being, he urges himself towards the Inner Realities which are unalterable and eternal. Forms, creeds, doctrines and dogmas, are to him simply human expressions of Everlasting Truth. He believes in no creed simply because it *is* a creed, but follows according to his best Judgement and knowledge whatever system suits him best in his search for God, and the attainment of the Divine Union.

Occultism makes full use of anything and everything which can possibly help even a single human being one step along the Path to ultimate Perfection. This Path has as many tracks as there are travellers, but it has only one destination. All states of consciousness are included within the range of Occultism, and the bond between its practitioners is that of Brotherhood to each other, and to the remainder of Creation besides. Occultism seeks not to separate human souls through sects and schisms, but to bring them together through tolerance into mutual love.

Epilogue

Within the history of mankind, Occultism has gone through three main periods of public opinion. Before the Christian era, it was revered as the wisdom of the Gods, possessed only by the Initiates. With the coming of the Church to power, it became feared and hated as "forbidden knowledge." When the rulership of the Church declined, and matter-of-fact materialism became the order of the day, Occultism was treated with good humoured contempt and ridicule, not to speak of an indifference born of a disinterest for anything beyond the physical plane. We are now working through that materialism, which has produced the most terrible wars that this world has ever known. Attitudes change but Occultism goes on, for it is as indestructible as the Universe. The time is approaching for another general swing-over amongst humanity, which will alter the direction of our mass-progress to an upward trend towards the Spirit from Whence we originated.

As this change occurs, Occultism will "come into its own." It will not do so as a rival of any existing creed, cult, or system, but as a fundamental in which all can unite, and continue their particular forms of expression in a progressive way through a common and Occult understanding. We are not yet quite ready for that change, but the advance guards are at work, and the progress is being steadily carried out. The heart of humanity cannot be changed by compulsion, and individuals must turn towards Truth of their own free accord. As they do so, the change will become self-evident, In the meantime guidance and help must go on in the best way possible.

Now I have tried (with some help) to give you some ideas and notions about Occultism, which will set your thinking about it in a practical and useful way. I am no Master or High Initiate, but only a sincere Occult student who sees Truth as I have written it, and firmly believes that what helped me, will also help others to build their own forms and expressions of the same Truths we cannot help but share together. Give me leave, therefore, to salute you in the traditional Occult fashion, and say with all my heart "The blessing of God Most High be with you, and

PERFECT PEACE PROFOUND!"

also published by The Sangreal Sodality Press

Shadow Tree Series
Volume 1

THE BOOK OF SELF CREATION

Jacobus G. Swart

'*The Book of Self Creation*' is a study guide for all who seek God within and who prefer to steer the course of their lives in a personal manner. The doctrines and techniques addressed in t his book will aid practitioners in the expansion of personal consciousness and spiritual evolution. Combining the principles and teachings of Kabbalah and Ceremonial Magic, the book offers step by step instructions on the conscious creation of physical life circumstances, such being always in harmony with the mind-set of the practitioner.

'The Book of Self Creation is a rich and resourceful workbook of practical kabbalah from the hands of a master kabbalist who is both compassionate and insightful.'
Caitlin Matthews, author of *Walkers Between the Worlds* and *Sophia, Goddess of Wisdom.*

The 'Shadow Tree Series' comprises a unique collection of Western Esoteric studies and practices which Jacobus Swart, spiritual successor to William G. Gray, has actuated and taught over a period of forty years. Regarding the author of this series, William Gray wrote 'It is well to bear in mind that Jacobus Swart is firstly and lastly a staunchly practicing member of the Western Inner Tradition and perforce writes from that specific angle alone. Moreover, he writes well, lucidly, and absolutely honestly.'

ISBN 978-0-620-42882-2   *Paperback*

also published by The Sangreal Sodality Press

Shadow Tree Series
Volume 2

THE BOOK OF SACRED NAMES

Jacobus G. Swart

'The Book of Sacred Names' is a practical guide into the meditational and magical applications of ancient Hebrew Divine Names. Perpetuating the tenets of traditional Kabbalists who recognised the fundamental bond between 'Kabbalah' and 'Magic,' Jacobus Swart offers step by step instructions on the deliberate and conscious control of personal life circumstances, by means of the most cardinal components of Kabbalistic doctrines and techniques—Divine Names!

The material addressed in this tome derives from the extensive primary literature of 'Practical Kabbalah,' much of which is appearing in print for the first time in English translation.

The 'Shadow Tree Series' comprises a unique collection of Western Esoteric studies and practices which Jacobus Swart, spiritual successor to William G. Gray and co-founder of the Sangreal Sodality, has actuated and taught over a period of forty years. Having commenced his Kabbalah studies in Safed in the early 1970's, he later broadened his 'kabbalistic horizons' under the careful guidance of the famed English Kabbalist William G. Gray.

ISBN 978-0-620-50702-8   *Paperback*

also published by The Sangreal Sodality Press

Shadow Tree Series
Volume 3

THE BOOK OF SEALS & AMULETS

Jacobus G. Swart

'The Book of Sacred Names' is a practical guide into the meditational and magical applications of ancient Hebrew Divine Names. Perpetuating the tenets of traditional Kabbalists who recognised the fundamental bond between 'Kabbalah' and 'Magic,' Jacobus Swart offers step by step instructions on the deliberate and conscious control of personal life circumstances, by means of the most cardinal components of Kabbalistic doctrines and techniques—Divine Names!

The material addressed in this tome derives from the extensive primary literature of 'Practical Kabbalah,' much of which is appearing in print for the first time in English translation.

The 'Shadow Tree Series' comprises a unique collection of Western Esoteric studies and practices which Jacobus Swart, spiritual successor to William G. Gray and co-founder of the Sangreal Sodality, has actuated and taught over a period of forty years. Having commenced his Kabbalah studies in Safed in the early 1970's, he later broadened his 'kabbalistic horizons' under the careful guidance of William G. Gray.

ISBN 978-0-620-59698-5 *Paperback*

also published by The Sangreal Sodality Press

Shadow Tree Series
Volume 4

THE BOOK OF IMMEDIATE MAGIC - PART 1

Jacobus G. Swart

'The Book of Immediate Magic - Part 1' perpetuates the fundamental tenets of "Self Creation" in which it is maintained that the "Centre" establishes the "Circumference," and that personal reality is emanated in harmony with personal "Will." Hence the first part of *"The Book of Immediate Magic"* comprises an enhance and expansion of the magical doctrines and techniques of *Kabbalah Ma'asit* (Practical Kabbalah) addressed in "The Book of Self Creation," "The Book of Sacred Names," and "The Book of Seals & Amulets." Jacobus Swart claims that working "Immediate Magic" is neither impossible nor difficult when we fully understand that consciousness is just one vast ocean, and that thoughts are the waves we make in it. It is all a matter of coordinating consciousness.

The 'Shadow Tree Series' comprises a unique collection of Western Esoteric studies and practices which Jacobus Swart, spiritual successor to William G. Gray and co-founder of the Sangreal Sodality, has actuated and taught over a period of forty years. He commenced his journey into the domain of Jewish Mysticism in the early 1970's investigating mainstream Kabbalah, later diversifying into the magical mysteries of Practical Kabbalah. He equally expanded his personal perspectives of Western Magical Traditions under the careful tutelage of his late mentor, the celebrated English Kabbalist William G. Gray.

ISBN 978-0-620-69313-4   *Paperback*

also published by The Sangreal Sodality Press

THE LADDER OF LIGHTS
(OR QABALAH RENOVATA)

William G. Gray

The Tree of Life works in relation to consciousness somewhat like a computer. Data is fed in, stored in associative banks, and then fed out on demand. The difference between the Tree and a computer, however, is that a computer can only produce various combinations of the information that has been programmed into it. The Tree, operating through the intelligent consciousness of living beings, whether embodied in this world or not, acts as a sort of Universal Exchange throughout the entire chain of consciousness sharing its scheme, and the extent of this is infinite and incalculable.

The Tree of Life is a means and not an end. It is not in itself an object for worship or some idol for superstitious reverence. It is a means, a method, a map and a mechanism for assisting the attainment of the single objective common to all creeds, systems, mysteries and religions—namely, the mystical union of humanity and divinity. With this end in view, this book is an aid to whoever desires to climb the Tree of Life.

'.....the most original commentary on basic Kabbalistic knowledge that I have read for God knows how many years.'
Israel Regardie

'.....beautifully presented and set in excellent marching order.....For one new to the subject, this is a fine text and an exceptionally lucid introduction to a veiled and meditative lore which is still being enlarged from year to year.'
Max Freedom Long (*Huna Vistas*)

ISBN 978-0-620-40303-0   *Paperback*

also published by The Sangreal Sodality Press

AN OUTLOOK ON OUR INNER WESTERN WAY

William G. Gray

'*An Outlook on Our Inner Western Way*' is a unique book. This is no dusty, quaint grimoire — it is a sane and simple method of true attainment for those who seek communion with their higher selves.

In this book, William Gray shows simply and lucidly, how to *live* the Western Inner Tradition. Tracing the cosmology of Western magic, he substantiates its vitality and urgency for our future.

William G. Gray is rated one of the most prolific — and controversial — occultists today. Blending keen insight, modern psychological models and an overall sense of practicality, his books have torn at the mouldy veils of so-called occult secrets, laying out a no-non sense foundation by which modern Western humanity may once again regain its precious magical soul.

ISBN 978-0-620-40306-1   *Paperback*

also published by The Sangreal Sodality Press

Sangreal Sodality Series
Volume 1

WESTERN INNER WORKINGS

William G. Gray

The '*Sangreal Sodality Series*' is a home study course comprising the fundamental text books of the Sangreal Sodality, that revives the instrumentality inherent in our western Tradition. The series makes available to us, in our own cultural symbolism, a way to enlightenment that we can practice on a daily basis.

'*Western Inner Workings*' provides a practical framework for the western student's psycho-spiritual development. Each day includes a morning meditation, a mid-day invocation, evening exercises, and a sleep subject. Incorporating symbols that are 'close to home,' these rituals increase consciousness in comfortable increments.

ISBN 978-0-620-40304-7   *Paperback*

also published by The Sangreal Sodality Press

A Beginners Guide to Living Kabbalah

William G. Gray

This compendium comprises six Kabbalistic works by William G. Gray, some of which are appearing here in print for the first time. The texts included in this compilation are ranging from the simplest introduction to the Spheres and Paths of the Kabbalistic Tree of Life system, to related meditation techniques and associated ritual magical procedures, to an advanced system of what could be termed 'inter-dimensional spiritual communication.'

The title 'A Beginners Guide to Living Kabbalah' is perhaps somewhat misleading, as this compilation equally contains works of an advanced nature, and the ritual and meditation techniques addressed in this tome, pertain to both beginners as well as advanced practitioners of 'Practical Kabbalah.'

ISBN 978-0-620-42887-3   *Paperback*

www.ingramcontent.com/pod-product-compliance
Lightning Source LLC
Chambersburg PA
CBHW021851300426
44115CB00005B/113